Purpose Crisis

Stop the Inner Struggle,
Find Your Life's Meaning
& Reveal The Magnificent
You Who's Ready To Be Seen

JuliAnn Stitick
The Personal Brand Expert

Purpose Crisis
Stop The Inner Struggle, Find Your Life's Meaning &
Reveal The Magnificent You Who's Ready to Be Seen

by JuliAnn Stitick
Copyright ©2018 and beyond by JuliAnn Stitick

Front Cover Image Photography by Stephanie Simpson.

Cover Design by Becky Rickett, Big Star Production Group.

Interior Design by Jeana DeShazer, New Journey Media.

Beverly Hills Publishing Firm.

ISBN: 978-1724998811

A special thank you...

My love note to Andréa Albright of Beverly Hills Publishing Firm for all of the care you have shown my vision. You have bolstered this mission and me along the way. Your commitment to this project has shown itself over and over. Here's to touching the lives of one billion and one women!

I love you dearly,

JuliAnn

This book is dedicated to you.
Fill your name in the blank

I believe in you. I believe you are capable of achieving all the dreams you have for your life. Even those dreams you keep hidden away because you don't believe they can ever be realized.

You are capable and powerful beyond words.

Table of Contents

Foreword

"We have not come into the world to be numbered; we have been created for a purpose; for great things: to love and be loved."
Mother Teresa

There is an emptiness that cannot be filled with money, influence, possessions, or even the highest form of recognition. You can see that it's missing from women when there is sadness behind their eyes, even when they have a smile on their face.

This void can only be filled when you find your real purpose in life. Regardless of how much money you make, how much prestige or popularity you garner, when you are not aligned with your purpose, you are missing a feeling of wholeness from within.

It is an unspoken undercurrent that permeates the crevices of the quietest moments when no one or nothing else is there to distract you from facing it head-on. It would be easy to brush it aside or turn a blind eye, and most of us do... for a while. But like every great ritual of awakening, finally and instantaneously, this crisis wakes us up from our hypnotic dream of mediocrity.

Now. This is your time. You cannot pretend or distract yourself from it any longer. No more time can go by without you bringing this to the forefront of your intentions. You are ready to have these conversations, so let me be the first to welcome you.

1

You have a purpose. Whether you are aware of it or not, there is something that is calling you to create it, become it, and live from this place of authenticity.

Time To Wake Up — We Are In A Crisis

"He who has a Why to live for
can bear almost any How."
Friedrich Nietzsche

Your purpose is the most profound meaning of what makes you unique, and ultimately different from every other person who has ever lived and will ever live again. If you're reading this book, then you're ready to face the beautiful, sobering truth that until you find out what your purpose is, you are living a lie.

Even if it's only a small fraction of a lie, it is still a lie. Like a drop of blood red dye that fills an entire swimming pool, even the tiniest trace of a lie will fester inside of you until it is confronted.

The lie of you not aligned with your purpose shows up in subtle ways depending on how great you are at disguising yourself from its impact. It may come out when you are speaking with your family or friends, and you notice that your tone of voice is constricted or harsh. It may show up when your alarm goes off in the morning and the idea of crawling out of bed one more day to face your work environment feels like torture. It may even show up when you are lying in bed at night, unable to fall asleep because something prevents you from drifting into a peaceful rest. However, or whenever it shows up for you, it is the time to eliminate all other possibilities of what it might be. You have come to a head-on collision with the reality that you are not living your best possible life.

Many people give motivational talks on finding your purpose or trusting your heart, but I'm daring to take it much further and address it more profoundly. The title of this book says it all— we are in a crisis.

It's a crisis because every day you spend not aligned and following your purpose is a day lacking the one thing that matters most. Radical self-expression and personal fulfillment can only be discovered when you know to the core of your soul who you are, who you are meant to be, right now… at this very moment.

There is no more waiting. There is nothing more to gain or be delivered from at this moment in time. You are perfectly whole with nothing to prove and nothing to win or lose. It is an awakening that is entirely natural. And every woman who has not discovered this within herself is depriving the world of her pure, inner beauty.

There are many different shades and sizes of real beauty, but one quality is always present--a light that radiates from within. There is a feeling of peace that surrounds her when she speaks, and a confidence that comes from purity. Unlike modern approaches to beauty where there is a "crown" for only one winner, this view of beauty is meant for everyone.

There is never a shortage of light for the sun to provide, just as there will never be too many women shining their brilliance of purpose. You will see this when a woman who is aligned with her most profound gifts lifts the world around her. It is a blessing, dare I say it, to be your most authentic version of yourself and to make no apologies for it.

We have to be aware of some of the dangers that are going to come from you living in your real, radically honest self-expression of YOU. It won't be easy - there are forces around you that will want you to go back to your hidden state. You have to be ready to see those forces ahead of time and face them head-on.

Eventually, through this process, you will stop caring about what other people think — this is great for you but hard for others to deal with when they realize what is happening. People who are used to you being a certain way are going to want to hold you in that cage. Don't let them. This is your chance to release your inner strength and break free from society's expectations of who you are supposed to be.

This is your chance to chisel away all the chains that have been holding you back from aligning with your one and only, God-given purpose.

My Purpose for Writing This Book

I went to dinner with some friends when I first began to write this book, and I said, *"Okay ladies, I want to do some market research with you because I'm writing this book about purpose"*. I asked each woman at the table to describe her purpose. It was exciting how each one had to really think about it. Not that they didn't know their purpose — most of them ultimately did, once I peppered them with questions — but it wasn't top of mind for them. That's what we want it to be. We want your purpose to be the beacon of your everyday life.

What makes me want to write this book about the *Purpose Crisis* happening to women today?

Well, the reason is twofold. One is because I know how confusing and even painful it can be, not knowing. It wasn't until I found my purpose that I began to truly love myself in a way I never had before. The second reason is, I've been developing personal brands for 22 years, and defining purpose is at the core of my work.

When I ask most women what their purpose is, they give me a generic answer. They tell me they are mothers or partners or philanthropists. It goes so much deeper than that because your purpose is not a role. What I have found is that your purpose, or the reason for which you were created, often comes out of what I call the *why of your why*. The *why of your why* is your pivotal story that ignited the passion you feel about your purpose and why you are driven to achieve it. It is a driving force to rid the world of hurt or lack in some arena of life that has impacted your personally. When women don't clearly understand their purpose, they are truly confused about who they are because their purpose is their true essence.

How does that impact your life?

The first rule of branding is that you want to be known for something concrete. The more specific, the better because people want to be able to put you in context. If we don't know our purpose, we don't have a point of reference from which to make choices and decisions. It manifests itself often when I work with women, and they are confused about their brand identity.

What often happens is these women have a variety of gifts. They might be great at serving people in their community. They might be skilled at math, and they might be interested in health and wellness. When it comes to their brand, they are not tying it all together with one-pointed focus. That causes confusion for them, and ultimately their customers. The same is true in life.

The golden thread that runs through all of those elements is a purpose. When you can identify that purpose, you can take all of those strengths, desires, hopes, and skillset, and point them back at the purpose. This combination of elements into one dominant force is the nexus of your brand.

It's the same in life because when we know our purpose, we see the intention of our soul. We can look at any situation or choice and ask ourselves if it is a step toward or away from that purpose, or what Neil Donald Walsh, one of my favorite authors, asks in *Conversations with God*, *"What does this have to do with the intention of my soul?"*

It's as simple as that.

After I heard Neil Donald Walsh speak at a conference, I came home from the event and was looking at my calendar for the upcoming week. There was one appointment in particular that felt wrong. It was with a gentleman who wanted to hire me to develop his brand. I was supposed to meet with him, and we were going to begin, but it just felt funky. Honey, you know that gut-feeling, right?

I had asked myself, *"What does this have to do with the intention of my soul?"* If I had taken him on as a client, it would have felt out of alignment for me, and that does not feed my purpose. So I decided to cancel the appointment because my gut knew he was not the type of client I wanted to work with.

Most of us know how important it is to have a purpose. It's like the North Star that will guide you in the right direction, so you will never be lost. When a woman is off purpose, she's making choices that are not in alignment with her soul, and it starts to manifest itself in different ways. Some women can have a full-on crisis, and some women aren't even aware that there is a problem. It shows up in other ways, like depression, anxiety, addictions, and relationship dysfunction.

You may have picked up this book because you are fully aware that you are in a *Purpose Crisis*. Or it may be that you have lost some of your spark and you feel "off your game." You are ready to face the fact that you are missing some level of fulfillment and meaning in your life. Wherever you are in this journey, you are safe with me. No matter what has brought you to this moment, you are ready to explore this on a deeper level. One thing I know for sure, you will not get this level of conversation anywhere else.

We are going to be traveling this journey together in three phases. I highly recommend that you get a special journal, one that makes your heart sing. In it, you can record your thoughts and responses to all the Action Steps I'll be assigning. This will be your Purpose Journal.

First off, we will look at what a purpose really is.

Secondly, we will walk a path together, so you can find your purpose.

And finally, we will make sure you can fuel your purpose for long-term success.

Here's the thing — this is the most important question you can ever ask yourself, "What is my purpose?" Yet you may not be asking it. That's why we are in a purpose crisis.

The point of this book and our journey together is for you to take the purpose challenge head-on, to awaken a bolder possibility for happiness and fulfillment in your life. You will experience more meaning than you've ever had before. And that begins with going deeper into the purpose conversation.

Broken Ankle Story

It was early May of 2018. My husband Joe and I were retreating at the Red Mountain Resort in southern Utah. After a couple of days, we had finally wound down and felt as serene as the landscape around us. This wellness retreat was a place for us to relax and get healthy.

One morning, the resort staff took us to the local medical center where we underwent an extensive health and wellness evaluation which tested our body fat, flexibility, CO_2 level, blood work--the works.

It had been a while since I had been exercising on a regular basis; I had just gotten out of the groove. Part of the program was two personal training sessions. The trainer and I immediately hit it off, and together we created a workout routine that I could do on my own. I was feeling good. I was enjoying the techniques he taught me for breathing deeply, relaxing my shoulders and holding an upright posture. I was beginning to get into the zone.

The third morning at the resort, I woke up early while Joe slept in. I made my protein shake and trekked down to the gazebo to meet my endurance hiking group. Joe decided to stay at the resort and work out in the gym for his daily exercise.

My hiking group hopped into a van and headed out to a remote location called Barrel Canyon, named after the barrel cactus, which is a very rare cactus and lives in very few places in the world. I wasn't sure if I was going to be able to keep up with the endurance group because I wasn't a regular hiker, but I thought I would give it a try. After we took off, the pace picked up very quickly. We were at high elevation, and I was getting winded and tired. I focused on opening my lungs so I could breathe deeply while my eyes were glued to the ground in front of me. We were on rocky terrain, and it took tremendous concentration to stay balanced.

We made it to the turning point, which was a vast, wide view over the ravine. It looked like something you would see in the Grand Canyon! We waited a few moments while taking a water break. A few of us took some photographs with our guides, and then we started to make our way back. I was talking about baking (my favorite hobby) with the guide who was right behind me. I was having so much fun, I decided it would be a great idea to join a hiking group when I returned home. I loved being outdoors, and I could take my dog Lily with me. Not 10 seconds after I made that decision, I stepped on a rock with my left foot. The stone rocked to the side, and in that instant, I broke my ankle.

Now, let me lay out the scene for you here. Because it was an extreme hike, it was impossible to get an emergency vehicle up the narrow, rocky path. I sat there in the only shade underneath a rock ledge, with my foot propped up on my hiking guide's backpack. Nick was a young man in his mid-20s and while we waited for the search and rescue team, we had a meaningful conversation about life and, as always, the coach in me popped up. I asked him what his purpose was. We began to talk more and more about purpose. He had hopes and dreams for his future that were very specific, and yet, the one missing piece was having a meaningful career that would allow him to get married and have a family. As we dug into his purpose, he realized he loved bringing people peace through nature. We discussed a couple of business ideas, and he seemed genuinely excited to begin creating the kind of future he wanted for his life.

The search and rescue team eventually showed up, and—drum roll please — they strapped me to a thick stretcher. Eight strapping firemen carried me down a rocky, cactus-filled embankment where the all-terrain vehicle (think dune buggy on steroids) was waiting. They secured my stretcher to the back of the vehicle, and because the terrain was so rough, it took us over an hour to travel only two miles back to the resort.

Imagine lying on a hard stretcher, strapped to the back of a monster vehicle, riding through bumpy, jagged terrain. Oh, and did I mention that most of my body was in the sun the whole time? I vividly remember a moment when I asked myself, *"How can I make this fun?"* This question allowed me to stop focusing on the embarrassment, (yes, I had put myself in a situation way beyond my ability, cue the canned laughter like on *I Love Lucy*. In this scenario, I am Lucy.) I started to see humor in this bizarre, unexpected situation.

In the midst of all of it, I decided to have fun. We joked, we talked about life, and we made it the best possible adventure it could be.

The all-terrain vehicle brought me to the resort emergency van where my hiking guides had been waiting for me. They ended up driving me to the urgent care center, but not before we stopped by a fast food restaurant for a medium drink with light ice (I will not tell you what it is because you might scold me).

The young guide and I exchanged phone numbers because he wanted me to let him know what the outcome of my injury was. Later, I texted him that my ankle was broken, which I believe surprised both of us. He responded by letting me know that as a result of our conversation, he had mended a relationship that had long-needed to be repaired. All it took was a ten-minute phone call. I knew right then that this broken ankle was worth the time we had to empower him to make that call.

Both hiking guides were young men that impressed me deeply. The next day I received a hand-written note card from each of them, along with a hiking flask. This simple gesture touched me.

Honestly, it was a beautiful day. It's in moments like the one with Nick I know the personal branding work I have been doing for 22 years, at some level, has led me to realizing my purpose. My purpose is helping people to find their purpose. It's about giving them strength and clarity to move beyond their *Purpose Crisis*. I'm here to help others move past their limiting beliefs that may be holding them back, in order to realize why they have been created.

It takes courage to claim your purpose. When you finally let go of all of the beliefs that have been cloaking you your entire life — like you're not good enough, or strong enough, or smart enough, or pretty enough, or tall enough — all those delusions fall away. You begin to see yourself like royalty, and you claim the purpose that has been inside of you all along. By aligning with your purpose, you are developing a purpose-driven brand whether you own a business or not.

I don't believe in manufacturing personal brands. They are not truthful or effective, nor will they connect with people. What's going to connect with people is the humanity of who you are. You are beautiful, and you are powerful. You are healthy, lovely, feisty, gritty, kind and gentle. You are loving, compassionate, open-hearted, fierce, committed, and you are so many other qualities that make you unique.

1

What Do You Want?

"There is nothing like a solid, steady aim, with an honorable purpose. It dignifies your nature, and ensures your success."
- Nelson Mandela

We live in a world where we are busier than ever, but when it comes to accomplishing our highest dreams and goals in life, we fall short. Why is this happening? We have modern tools for productivity, and nonstop technology alerting us for every appointment. We have more ways to entertain ourselves than ever before, yet nothing is filling that void. We are missing the essential sense of being satisfied inside of our soul. We are missing out on living our purpose.

If you've ever been to a personal development seminar or read a self-help book, you know that one of the keys to accomplishing your priorities in life is to focus on being productive versus being busy. Unfortunately, it is rare to meet someone who is genuinely achieving their highest purpose in life. Most of us are just busy and not productive when it comes to the things that matter most.

Busy Vs. Productive

According to an article in *Forbes* magazine, *"Busy people tend to be over-thinkers, and they have an incredible ability to expand their tasks to the amount of time they have available."*

Being busy is the old-fashioned way of working that keeps your schedule jam-packed while you have to multitask to keep all the balls in the air. As researchers learn more about the science of the brain and how it works best, it turns out this style of jumping between tasks significantly decreases your brain's ability to focus. It also creates more stress in your mind and body. This is where I would clang symbols to get your attention.

According to *Forbes*, *"Being productive is the core of every high-level achiever in the game. Whether its Warren Buffett, Oprah Winfrey, Tony Robbins or Jeff Bezos, they all have mastered their time management and became extremely productive and results-driven."* The most productive people in the world have clear goals, and they focus on one thing — the most important thing — so they can harness their mind's ability to eliminate all the noise and distractions.

While we are going through this journey, I am going to ask you to focus on your one goal — to get absolute, unresolved clarity on your purpose. When you shut off the distractions, you will have more thinking capability with less stress.

When I am sitting down with a client who is ready to go on this journey, we start with the vision--The

Purpose Question: *"What do you want for your life?"*

It's important to get very specific about what you want. What that means is looking way out at the vision. Not the vision you think you should have because anybody can have that. It's the vision of what you would dream if no obstacles or limitations were holding you back. It's the response a child would give before the big world impacted her imagination and belief in herself. When you know what this vision is for you, there are no rules. You dream as big and high as you can. No other voices get to vote.

Allow your imagination to explore in this first exercise with me now.

ACTION STEP: The Unlimited You Exercise

Complete the Unlimited You Exercise and note your answers in your Purpose Journal.

The Unlimited YOU Exercise

We want to describe each of these in detail:

1. What are your ideal relationships like? (partner, kids, family, friends, etc.) Writing down an answer rather than just thinking it through will give you the most significant impact in finding your purpose. In other words, write it down doll.

2. What is your perfect environment? (home, work, free time, etc.)

3. What is your health like? (energy levels, sleeping, mental clarity, happiness levels, etc.)

4. What is your business or career like in your perfect vision? (how much income, how many employees, work from home or commute to an office, etc.)

5. What are your hobbies? (free time activities, travel, community involvement, sports, and recreation, etc.)

6. What are you doing for fun? (dinner dates, hanging out with your friends, family time, creative art projects, etc.)

7. How are you contributing to the world? (philanthropy, charity, volunteering, non-profit, fundraising, etc.)

JuliAnn Stitick

The Personal Brand Expert

PurposeCrisis.com

Okay now that you have identified your list of priorities living from the highest ideal of YOU, we are going to create a "Day in the Life of You."

While you remain in the imagination process, answer the following questions in your Purpose Journal. What does a typical day look like for Unlimited You?

- What time do you wake up? What do you think about when you first wake up?
- How do you spend your morning?
- Do you practice exercise and health rituals? What are they exactly?
- What foods nourish your body?
- What are you doing to contribute to the world?
- Who do you interact with during your work day?
- Describe your work environment
- What time do you stop working?
- How do you spend your evenings? What's your ritual for winding down?
- What time do you go to sleep? What do you think about as you fall asleep?

How was that exercise for you? Many people have doubts that creep into their thinking, *"But I couldn't have this,"* or *"I couldn't achieve that."* If you noticed any of those doubts coming up for you, you are entirely normal. Like most of my clients, you will find you have to free yourself of your self-doubt in order to do this exercise. This is why we are starting here on this journey together.

Most women never permit themselves to express their dreams. Just like a muscle that gets stronger every time you use it, your purpose muscle will get stronger too. In case you haven't noticed, strong muscles are trending. (I don't know that for a fact, but it sounds good to me).

We have to start with the possibility of creating your life as if you had no barriers and no self-doubt. That's where we can discover the truth of what your dream really is.

Regardless of how easy or hard you found this exercise, we are going to let go of it for now. We will be revisiting this same exercise at the end of our journey together so that you can see the differences that will occur through this process.

Nancy's Story

Nancy initially hired me as an image expert because she was branding herself as a food personality on YouTube. She had run a successful PR firm for nearly 20 years, and was the food editor for a local magazine. Nancy hired me because she saw a photo of me with a friend of hers on her brand shopping day. As Nancy and I began our work together, she realized I was going to bring a lot more to the table than simply guiding her on her image.

We began by diving into her brand identity. As she described her work to me, I said, *"You know, you don't seem very excited about this."*

She sat back, *"I guess I'm not."*

"What would you want to do if you could do absolutely anything?"

She quickly replied, *"Well, it has to have something to do with food."* And then she hesitated.

So I probed, *"What else...?"*

Nancy hesitatingly responded, *"Well, I kind of like photography."*

"Great. You can become a food photographer."

Her immediate reaction was, *"But I don't know anything about photography."*

My response, *"That's not a problem. You can learn."*

A smile filled her entire face, *"Really?"* she questioned.

"Absolutely. Is this something you want to go after?" Her reply was a resounding, *"Yes!"*

That conversation was the turning point in her life and career. Nancy thought about it for a couple of weeks and decided she was really going to go for it.

During her next coaching session, we crafted a Facebook post that announced her intention to begin her food photography business. She was nervous about it and we talked it through, *"What is your concern?"* I asked this to go deeper into her hesitation.

She replied, *"I don't know... people are going to think I'm crazy."* She was experiencing a lot of the same feelings that I and many other clients of mine have when their hopes and dreams become more visible. We are afraid to let ourselves be seen because others may not like it or approve. What if people judge our dreams?

You know what I say to that? Who cares? Because it's not them that's judging; it's you judging yourself. Let me say that again. It's you judging you. You might be judging yourself because of your upbringing. You might be judging yourself because you were raised hearing that your brother was the artistic one and you weren't. It may be that you had a critical parent who never supported you. There are so many reasons why we judge ourselves. To awaken to your true purpose in life, you must release that judgment.

It's a big moment when you begin to claim who you truly are inside. What you intrinsically already know.

I helped Nancy craft that Facebook post announcing her photography business, and she hemmed and hawed about pushing the post button. I enthusiastically said, *"Push the button!"* She did, and, as you might guess, she was flooded with positive feedback.

That boosted her spirits and confidence and paved the way to launch her business. Deep down inside, everyone wants a success story; those who matter will want to support you in creating yours.

Just a year later, Nancy was running a wildly successful food photography business, and had been published in USA Today on "National Ice Cream Day." Today, she couldn't be happier.

The moment we step into our purpose is the moment when we say *"NO"* to all the judgment that has held us back in the past. Whether from ourselves or others, when we are allowing judgment to rule our actions, we are preventing our true gifts from being shared.

The sooner we say *"YES"* to our purpose, the sooner we are going to feel fulfilled and make the world a better place. What Nancy realized is that her purpose is to spread meaning by sharing the beauty of food to remind families and friends to create community over the dinner table. That's her way of contributing.

What are the chains that are holding you back?

ACTION STEP: Notice Your Self-Judging

Some chains have stopped you from being the brightest version of yourself. Together, we will break free from those chains. In your Purpose Journal write down the ways you are judging yourself.

2

What Is Your Purpose?

"Many persons have a wrong idea of what constitutes true happiness. It is not attained through self-gratification but fidelity to a worthy purpose."
Helen Keller

Many women make the mistake of thinking they will discover their purpose through some external force or from somewhere outside of themselves. They look outward to seek the validation that can only be found within.

As part of aligning our minds to believe that we are on our purpose and deserving to find our purpose, we need to identify the emotions associated with this journey.

It's crucial that you look for these signs as we travel this path. I see too many women give up before the miracle happens. They believe they are supposed to have this jaw-dropping moment that rips away all doubt and fear, but rarely does your true purpose show up like that. Before you may ever have the "ah-ha" awakening that THIS is why you have been born, you will feel emotions that are subtler to show you that you are on your path. It's up to you, the one who is taking this inner journey, to become aware of the subtle and vital cues that will prove that this process is working.

Keys to Staying Motivated

Motivation can be complicated if you choose to make it that way. I like to keep it simple. My favorite definition of motivation comes from a past mentor who said, *"Motivation is the movement of emotions."* I especially like this definition because it gives me something to grasp. I can observe my emotions as they dance around and move about inside me.

When you are traveling on this journey to discover your purpose, always tune in to your feelings. The key is to harness these emotions to make sure they are working for you instead of against you.

Your emotions will act as light posts guiding you away from the tumultuous waves of the *Purpose Crisis* and onto the stable, grounded rock of truth. It starts with feelings like — inspiration, happiness, hope, excitement, love, bliss, wonder, curiosity, and positivity. Experiencing these emotions is a sign that you are moving in the right direction — towards your purpose. It's waiting for you and signaling you with emotional cues.

According to an article in *Inc. Magazine*[1], if you state these emotions as part of who you are, then you will feel higher levels of this motivation. When you feel these emotions, state them in a compelling way that turns them into your identity. "I am hopeful. I am curious."

You want to do the exact opposite when you encounter negative emotions. When you feel emotions that bring you down — feeling stuck, depressed, angry, frustrated, tired, overwhelmed, bored, lonely — you want to state these in a way that removes them from your identity. For instance, you will want to say, *"I'm feeling sad"* instead of *"I am sad."* Just this simple reframe of the words removes you from identifying with this negative emotion.

Here's a quote from the article, *"In other words, if you want to become more successful, train your brain to:*

- Characterize negative emotions as what you're doing rather than what you're feeling or who you are.

- Characterize positive emotions as who you are rather than what you're doing or feeling."

Being aware of how you do or don't identify with your emotions is going to be an essential tool for staying motivated on this road to finding your purpose. When you experience emotions that stir positive feelings inside of you, hold onto them as this is the new YOU. This is the new identity that is pulling you closer to your purpose.

ACTION STEP: "I Am" Framework

In your Purpose Journal write down five positive emotions with the "I am" framework.
Now, be honest with yourself. Are you feeling some negative emotions right now as we go through this process together? There is nothing wrong with expressing your negative emotions as long as you do not identify with them.

ACTON STEP: "I Am Feeling/Doing" Framework

In your Purpose Journal write down five negative emotions with the *"I am feeling"* or *"I am doing"* framework.

Go Deeper Into Your Purpose Discovery Process

Now that we have gotten clear on what you want, it's time to go deeper.

The second question is, *"What Is Your Purpose?"*

I live very simply. Everything is sparse and tidy in my home. That's what helps open my mind and fosters creativity. When I'm in open space, I can explore deeper. That's how we are going to travel on this journey together. With simple, clear-cut questions, you will find the deeper meaning to your life's purpose.

Okay, so what is your purpose? Have a little fun with me now. I'll have you express your purpose now and then again at the end of this book. It will grow. You'll see. I'm excited for you.

ACTION STEP: What Is Your Purpose?

In Your Purpose Journal write the answer to the question, "What is your purpose?"

Whatever you wrote down is perfect for where you are in this process. As we continue, we are going to go deeper into this question.

My Journey

I've been married to Joe for 24 years. In mid-2017, I moved out of our house and rented an apartment in the neighboring town. We were getting ready to start a major remodel on the house, and it didn't make sense for me to be living in the chaos of the rebuild while running my business. I most certainly would not have been able to work from home. Joe, on the other hand, wanted to stay home while the construction was going on so he could oversee the progress.

It was also an opportune time in our relationship for us to have some space because things were breaking down. Joe was wholeheartedly involved with the house remodel; whereas I had finally admitted to myself and everyone that I did not want to remodel our home. I wanted to downsize and simplify. Joe's heart was committed to the remodel so I compromised. I knew it wouldn't work for me to live for months on end in construction chaos so I moved out.

Once I moved away from my home where I'd lived the last two decades of my life, I realized I was in crisis. I had completely lost myself, trying my whole life to please other people and control circumstances so I would feel safe. Safe from someone taking advantage of me. Safe from someone betraying me. Safe from someone hurting me. I reflected on how hard I had been working to control my life, my family, my world. Once I was on my own, the truth hit me hard. I realized that I had never really trusted others. Trust doesn't always come easily for me. You may relate.

What I'm going to share now is about a personal journey that was facilitated by mentors and professionals when necessary. It is not something that happened overnight. From the bottom of my heart, I encourage you to ask for help and hire professionals when you need their support. This process takes time and patience and courage and you, my dear, have plenty of courage.

In my move away from home, I stripped away the familiar surroundings and relationship that had protected me for decades. I built my world anew from the ground up. You could say I had moved from a construction zone into an internal construction zone. For the first time ever, I was living alone.   There were many lonely, painful moments that forced me to face myself and what was missing from my life. I had been so busy raising a family and tending to the happiness of others, I had not taken the time to discover myself and what mattered most to me. I was in a place of transition and crisis and, while I held fast to my faith, I was still missing a big piece of me. Why had I been created? What was special about me? How could I be useful in my own unique way?

There were times I was angry and blamed myself and others for this emptiness I was feeling. As I delved into self-discovery I knew it would be essential to let those feelings go so I could see myself and my purpose clearly. I had been guiding others in this self-discovery process for years and it was time to face myself.

The work I did (and continue to do) has refined me in a way that heightens my empathy, compassion, and gifts. I have insight that I might never have had. It is because of that critical work, I'm able to help other women fight for who they are meant to be. I have lived through the struggle, and I am now able to express what I love, what I feel, and what I want. I want that for you, too.

Forgiveness

"If we want to love, we must learn how to forgive."
Mother Teresa

Forgiveness is a conscious and decisive choice to let go of feelings of resentment or vengeance towards someone who has hurt you. Forgiveness is not forgetting, condoning or excusing the act, the behavior, or the person. Forgiveness can and does repair relationships, but it does not mean you must reconcile with someone who has seriously hurt you.

To begin with, I want you to forgive one tiny thing. Sit back for a moment and think of someone you have unresolved anger towards. But make sure the hurt is a minor one. It needs to be something small. It could be someone who cut you off on the road or some unthinking comment from an acquaintance. By keeping it small, it will assure your success in today's challenge.

ACTION STEP: Baby Step Forgiveness of Others

Close your eyes and think of her/him/them (whoever is your 'subject matter'). Picture them in your mind as if they were in the same room with you. I know this may not sound fun at the moment, but bear with me. By the end of this exercise, you will see forgiveness in a new light and quite possibly be free from negative emotions and actions that have been hurting you for a long while. Once you have your

36

'subject' in mind, and you can see them sitting in the same room as you, read on.

The first step in forgiving is deciding to forgive. We think we need to work our way up to forgiving, but the truth is the decision to forgive comes first, and then you do the work to sustain and finally release it.

There's also a precursor to forgiveness, and that is making a choice NOT to let a resentment form. Recently I was chatting with a woman who unknowingly said something very hurtful to me. My child spirit withered under her judgmental remark. Ouch. I could have harbored the comment, simmered on why she might have said it or began to look for other ways she was inconsiderate. There have been many times I've gone down that path, but this was not one of them.

That day, in an instant, I decided to forgive. I forgave her and then for extra measure I blessed and released her. That's not to say that there are not more layers, but it did mean I had taken that first and most significant action. I am still on the journey and when another layer needs forgiveness, I go back to these simple steps:

1. Decide
2. Forgive
3. Bless and release

Forgiveness frees us from the negative charges within our relationships and within ourselves. Living life from a place of forgiveness reduces feelings of tension, anger, depression, and fatigue. A 2005 Journal of Behavioral Medicine Study reported, *"The present study suggests that this pathway most fully mediates the forgiveness-health relationship. Thus, health consequences of lack of forgiveness may be carried by increased levels of negative emotion."*

Equally as important as the stress on our health is the emotional and spiritual toll it takes when we hold onto anger or resentment. Repeat this process over and over until you feel free of the negative charge.

Recall the person you visualized at the beginning of this section. Close your eyes and bring them back to your awareness. Picture them looking into your eyes. Tell them you forgive them. Look at them from a place of doing the best they can do given their life circumstances and personal toolbox. Then, bless them and release all anger towards them. Pray for them to thrive in their life- their relationships, health, prosperity, and happiness.

Hopefully, you can release the negative energy, but if you don't right away, rinse and repeat until you do. If you don't feel like praying for them, pray for the willingness to pray for them. It's the action that's the magic.

Repeat this process over and over until you feel free.

1. Decide
2. Forgive
3. Bless and release

Once you have accomplished forgiveness for one tiny thing, you can move on to another. Working each day to forgive something new or something old will begin to free you from the negative emotions associated with lack of forgiveness.

Now let's talk about forgiving ourselves. That's a hard one, isn't it? For some reason, we are the hardest people to forgive, or is it just me?

I've made a lot of choices that I wouldn't make again with the wisdom I have now. In the past, I allowed those choices to define me. Forgiving myself for those choices has removed the shame, so now I can say those choices refined me.

When we think about forgiving ourselves, we think it needs to be more complicated, but it doesn't. We are going to use the same steps we used in the forgiving another person exercise above, except now we are also going to add an extra step to make sure it sticks.

1. Make a decision
2. Forgive
3. Bless and release
4. Ask for help

When we go through the process of forgiving ourselves, we need to make sure we reach out for support from others who love us. It's easy to fall back into the self-defeating loop of sabotage. By asking for help, you are giving yourself the greatest gift of healing. You are saying, *"I'm worth it"*. This process of forgiveness strengthens your self-esteem and gives you more clarity to focus on your purpose.

Forgive because you want to embody love without the sharp edges of holding a grudge. You want your sunlight to shine through like a freshly cleaned windowpane rather than a muddy piece of glass.

Now, find a moment in the day when you can forgive yourself for one small thing. You may have made a mistake and need to give yourself some grace. Remember, you are doing the best you can, considering your circumstances and experiences.

ACTION STEP: Baby Step Forgiveness

At the end of your day come back to this question, *"How do you feel about your decision to forgive?"* Write about this in your Purpose Journal.

- Who is one person you can forgive?
- Are you willing to forgive them at this moment?
- How can you view him/her as needing your grace?
- How about YOU? What do you want to forgive yourself for?

- Are you deciding right now to forgive yourself?
- How can you see YOURSELF as needing your grace?

Letting Go of Shame and Judgment

Pep Talk: Hello Friend. Today is a day of releasing negativity and hurt. When you let go of anger and pain, you will live in a place of kindness and loving care. Let go of the negativity and the physical and emotional stress of holding resentment. It's time to let it go, releasing it to the wind. Letting it float out to sea, never to be seen again. You are worth living a life of free from your self-imposed chains.

I look at shame and judgment as darkness. It closes people up behind walls they build. They can't see the good in themselves. I know this darkness firsthand. I know that there could be a thousand things right with me, yet if there's one experience that triggers my shame, it closes in on me. I can't see the multitude of positive qualities about myself. Is it just me?

When you let go, you will be able to live in a place of forgiveness, peace, calm, and freedom. You will feel lighter, more grounded, and open. Letting go helps you to hold your head up, put your shoulders back, and open up to realize the precious being that you are. Let your beautiful spirit shine.

Kristen's Story

I met Kristen on the first day of a conference. She had purchased my book, *The Total Package: 5 Keys to a Profitable Personal Brand* (available on Amazon). The next morning, she walked up to me, and said, *"I just read the first three chapters of your book, and I want to hire you. I don't have absolute certainty about what you're going to do for me, but I know I want to work with you."*

Today, that relationship has evolved, but in the beginning, she connected with my personal story in the first three chapters of that book. She knew she could trust me because I understood her. It was because I was transparent and real that our souls connected.

That is an incredibly important example of why you must be yourself and be authentic in your branding. When others feel they know you, you build instant trust and credibility.

Kristen knew that she wanted to be more visible, but she was afraid. She owns two highly successful businesses, and she was working up to 80 hours a week to keep them going. As a single woman the primary focus of her life was her career.

What I think she saw in the first three chapters of that book is that I am nurturing to my clients, and she wanted to cultivate a more nurturing relationship with herself.

We started working together specifically on her image and began with these three questions:

1. Who was instrumental in teaching you how to dress and care for yourself?
2. Was it done with love, or was it done with judgment and dysfunction?
3. Was it done by someone who knew what the heck they were talking about?

Like some of my clients, she did not have a great role model in her mother, and it impacted her greatly.

Those early childhood messages made her stay small and hidden, and it drove her to seek her validation from external sources instead of inside of herself. This seeking for her true identity ultimately drove her to start two businesses and achieve great success on the surface level of fulfillment. At the same time, she was missing her purpose because her career was where she had been finding her identity. Because of this, she wasn't taking care of herself.

We focused heavily on self-care. Once she started looking at herself as needing nurture, things began to change. Indeed, her inner and her outer image changed. She looked healthier and was happier. Her staff was commenting that she was changing for the better. She was wearing clothes she felt beautiful in. She was getting her hair and her nails done on a more regular basis. She tried a new hairstyle and color, updated her makeup, and played a little more freely with her accessories. Her business revenue increased in both companies, and she related that directly to her new-found focus on self-care.

This outward expression all came from the work we did in recognizing what was keeping her image small. It was the criticism and negativity she experienced growing up that was keeping her hidden. She began to identify the behaviors she did not want for herself. These behaviors were unconscious choices that she was making on autopilot. The mindset, the language she was using, her attitude about life, and even the way she was dressing did not fit who she wanted to be in her vision. She began to recognize that she had a choice to change those things.

One of my favorite sayings is *"the feelings follow the actions."* Once Kristin began to take the step of putting her self-care at the forefront of her mind, her life started to change for the better.

Here are some of the ways that Kristen began to prioritize her self-care:

- getting her hair done on a more regular basis
- treating herself to a manicure regularly
- updating her look
- eating more nutritious foods
- drinking more water
- exercising on a regular basis
- getting enough sleep

- quieting her mind with meditation
- using essential oils in her home and work environment
- taking time for adventure and fun
- asking for help

These are all actions that a woman who values herself will take. By taking these actions, she begins to believe that she is the woman she's always known was inside. These actions lead to appreciating herself.

Kristen went on to go through my high-level Total Package Plus program. In that program, we covered five different elements of her purpose-driven brand experience:

1. Brand Identity
2. Brand Image
3. Language: written, spoken and nonverbal
4. Online Presence
5. Customer Experience

Wherever you are in your journey, the simple action of reading this book and doing The Action Steps will help you develop a new identity. It is an identity that is aligned with your core, the woman you want to become.

3

Tickle Your Tingle

"As far as we can discern, the sole purpose of human existence is to kindle a light in the darkness of mere being."
Carl Jung

The Missing Piece - What You Can't See?

If you're like many women, you may not even know what your purpose is. That's where we need to go deeper and look into what's missing. What is this missing piece? I call this, Tickle Your Tingle.

What do I mean by tickle your tingle? First, I have to describe what the tingle is. The tingle is that feeling you get in the pit of your stomach and feels a little bit like butterflies. It can come over you at the strangest times, but it is a feeling that gets your attention. I get this tingle when my clients see a glimpse of their greatness. It is this bright light of who they are undimmed by life's experiences, a light breaking through in their eyes as they see themselves anew.

Tickling your tingle is taking actions to nurture yourself, your environment, and others around you so your bright white light can begin to shine.

I was at a speaking engagement in Toronto about ten years ago, and there were about a thousand women in the audience. When I did my presentation, I asked the audience to raise their hand if they thought they had a light in them. Only 50% of the room raised a hand.

I said, *"Everybody put your hand up please because even if you don't believe you have a light inside you, I do. If that's something that you can hold on to, you will begin to see yourself as light. Until you see it, then I am happy to be the stake in the ground for you."*

I then asked everyone to raise a hand again, and more like 85% of the room raised their hands this time. Then I asked them to put their hands down.

I followed up with, *"How many of you think you can shine your light brighter than you're shining it today?"* I'm happy to say that the entire room raised their hands. It was an acknowledgment that they did have this light inside of them — a hope.

For some women, this is like a missing piece, something that's missing inside of them. If you are not able to acknowledge this light and your purpose, and you don't know what to do, ask yourself this question, *"Is there a possibility I have a light and a purpose?"*

If you don't even know where to start or where to find that, I want you to guess. Yes, seriously. Let me explain.

I think a lot of women are waiting for a big booming voice to tell them, *"This is it!"* ... but it rarely happens that way. Most women I know discover their true purpose over years of self-exploration and personal inquiry. They take risks and experiment over and over before they finally find their deepest mission in life.

In some ways, I would say we're all still really looking for our purpose. Even if someone knows what their purpose is, there may still be some uncertainties about how to move forward with it. Some people know their purpose, but they get stuck, asking, *"How do I infuse this purpose into my life?"*

When I'm working with a client, we take it on as a theoretical question. We ask as though we already know the answer. When I ask them to tell me their purpose, and they don't know the answer, I'll respond with, *"Well, if you had to guess, what would you say it is?"*

Typically, I get a watered-down answer because women are afraid to put their hopes and dreams out there. It's scary for women to speak their dreams into reality. The details are different for everyone, but the fear seems to be the same. Through their life experiences or upbringing, those dreams and hopes become shadowed with doubt.

Don't get me wrong, I'm not trying to be morbid here, and I'm not into blaming our families for our fate. I believe that each of us has our destiny. You may agree that each of us has the power to make choices for our own life. No matter how far down the road we have gone, how far we have fallen, we can get back up. We can make a decision and ask for help. We can forgive, we can heal, and we can move on.

If you're stuck asking yourself, *"What is my purpose?"*, and you don't know the answer, ask yourself again in a different way. If you had to guess what your purpose is, what would you guess?

Fuel the Tingle

Now that you've begun to find your tingle, it's important to make sure that you continue to throw fuel into the fire. Many women allow their desire to fade, and then it becomes harder to get back on track.

As you tap into your purpose, you want to fuel it and set it up for sustainable success. To fuel the hope and the vision of this purpose requires nurture.

When I moved into my apartment (or 'she shack'), I learned how important it was for me to create a peaceful and serene environment. This makes me feel loved, nurtured, and cocooned. It gives me a safe place where I can recharge and then go out to be more powerful in the world.

I'm one of those people who is an outgoing introvert. I love people, I love being with people, and I love connecting with people. When it comes down to where I feel most comfortable, I'd rather have a one-on-one conversation than be in a big group any day.

My home has to be a place of quiet. I haven't watched the news or read the news report for years now. I am living in the bliss of the moment. I live in the now and focus on the things I have control over, which is what is right in front of me. It takes work and commitment.

Through my journey in life, I have developed systems, blueprints, timelines, and checklists to organize my environment in order to create the healthiest, happiest, fullest life in all areas. This doesn't happen by accident. It requires planning and consistency. I'm going to be sharing my self-care rituals in upcoming chapters so that you can create the most optimal environment to fuel your purpose.

It's important to see where we've come from and where we are going on this journey. So far we've identified what chains may have kept you from seeing your purpose. Now that we have this clarity, we're expanding deeper into it. We need to be honest with ourselves and see that it is going to take a commitment to assure these chains don't come back because they will form again if you're not consciously removing them.

I'm here to hold your hand through every step of the way. It's my role to prepare you for what is going to happen, and give you the tools you need to avoid falling back into a Purpose Crisis again.

The Blueprint to Be Extraordinary

When someone says, *"JuliAnn, you always seem so together and it looks effortless!"* First, I sincerely thank them. If someone pays you a compliment and you don't receive it openly and willingly, you are not appreciating them. It's like they've just handed you a gift, and you placed it on a shelf unopened.

I thank them, receive the compliment, and then I chuckle inside because that effortless presence takes LOTS of effort. Life is in session for each of us, and I have found ways to fuel myself and my purpose so I can thrive through the adversity. What I've done is create a blueprint to be extraordinary.

I'm going to pull back the curtains and show you my roadmap for success. First, you're going to change on the inside, and then the outside will transform. People are going to see you differently. They're going to see you as radiant and alive. Most importantly, you will feel renewed!

I'm going to share resources, checklists, and everything you need to take this step-by-step. This is a system to fabulosity (I just made that word up)!!

Gila's Story

Gila is the owner of Dog Is Good. She is the co-founder, along with her husband, John. They've been in business for ten years. Dog Is Good is a lifestyle brand for dog lovers. Their goal is to make you feel the way you do the first two minutes after you get home when your dog is greeting you.

Gila used to be a teacher. When she and her husband relocated, she had to let go of her teaching position. In recent years, they've achieved great success and fulfillment from starting up Dog Is Good, but Gila has always missed teaching.

She took part in my "VIP Ultimate Brand Experience" where we mapped out her personal brand strategies and vision. As she talked about her company and all of the different revenue streams they were generating, there was a slight emptiness in her tone of voice. As we began to get further into the conversation, it became clear that she was missing some fulfilling component in her work.

Gila is also the author of the book *Fur Covered Wisdom*, which bridges inspirational lessons of what people can learn from dogs. In it, she's full of wisdom, insight, and transparency. Every time she mentioned *Fur Covered Wisdom*, her eyes lit up.

They glowed as she told me about one of their new programs that allowed her to be in a teaching or coaching role for her exhibitors. However, she kept putting *Fur Covered Wisdom* on the back burner because it wasn't something that was driving her revenue.

What it came down to was— she was missing teaching. The Dog is Good business itself was meaningless to her if she wasn't able to add this teaching component.

At the end of her VIP day, we looked at the notes we'd taken on poster size post-it's stuck to the walls. There was one word that stood out. The word was Teacher.

It's important to share that sometimes the *Purpose Crisis* doesn't show up as a breakdown, or divorce, or addiction, or depression. Sometimes it can be like Gila. Even though she was having success, she wasn't experiencing fulfillment of the soul. Gila walked away that day looking at every element of her business in a new way, asking herself, *"How can I infuse teaching into this component?"*

Today, Gila is taking her gift, joy, and passion as a teacher and soaking her purpose in a brand that spreads positivity, love, and animal connectedness. As a result, Gila is glowing and radiant and alive!!

Lovingly Taking Space for Yourself

When I first got together with Joe, I was 26 years old and I immediately jumped into the world of a 46-year-old man. He came from an affluent world, and I did not. I felt the need to show up and act like those in his peer group. Not that he had that expectation of me, I just did it. I shifted to be able to feel "part of" his world. Without knowing it, I lost what could have been some very formative growth.

One of the things that I have always known is that I am a butterfly inside. I am a dandelion that you blow in the wind. I am a flower child at heart and a free spirit. I'm super, super creative, but that needed to be buttoned up so that I could fit into the society that I thought I was supposed to fit into when I married Joe. My desire to fit in ended up squelching my creativity for years.

As I've matured my creativity has grown even more powerful. It has bloomed. It wasn't until I got into my own space that I realized how much I love the freedom to create.

During that time I softened my image. I let more of my hair's natural color show (but that's just for today... who knows what tomorrow holds). I allowed a little bit of Bohemian style into what was a more conservative corporate look.

My brand image became more comfortable because I decided that I wanted to be more comfortable in life, period. If that means I don't want to put on a pair of Spanx (or two) to be able to wear the dress that I think I'm supposed to wear, then I'm not going to do it anymore.

My clothing style is just a reflection of the fact that I've relaxed into who I am as a woman. It's not just about feeling confident, but more importantly, relaxing into who I am on the inside and it's a beautiful way of being. Each day, when I wake up and realize there is nothing to prove, I find myself.

If you're going through a transition, or a life circumstance is disrupting your status quo, that in itself can be an experience of self-learning and growth. There's something to be seen in the exploration of the *not knowing*. We can look at the *not knowing* as terrifying, or we can see it with the hope that we're growing, we're changing, and letting our wings out.

Still Discovering Myself

What does it mean to me that I am still discovering myself? Even someone who's done all this self-work, personal development — what does it mean that there's always more to explore?

When I get asked that question, it tickles my tingle.

I am so excited about the continued growth that I'm having and will continue to have for the rest of my life. I answered a questionnaire recently asking what age I plan to retire. Are you kidding me? I'm not going to retire... ever! I'm always going to be doing something.

Even when I'm an old woman, and I'm mentoring young women, I want to continue to grow. I want to keep going to feel pain. I want to keep going to feel joy. Only then will I know I'm evolving. To stop growing is to die. Staying committed to growth is a feeling of wonder and hope. It is a knowing within that says, *"I've come this far, let's see how things are going to get better and better and better."*

The more women we have in our culture who stay true to this ever-expanding, never-reaching-the-end attitude, the better the world is going to be.

There are many different ways to ensure we are still growing along our path and I'm going to share some of my favorites.

Sing From Your Heart

One thing that brings me the most joy is singing as if my heart is going to burst out of my chest. Many women silence their voices because they don't think they sound good enough, but this is a tragedy. Whether you are in the shower or your kitchen, sing out loud and don't hold back. When you are driving in your car, crank up your favorite song and belt it out. Singing has been proven to increase dopamine in the brain which is the novelty hormone that makes us feel peaceful and content. That's why singing is one of the best medicines for happiness.

When you allow yourself to sing it also brings a profound sense of connecting to yourself and allowing your inner light to shine. Stop the self-judgment and the ridicule. Remember back to a time when you would sing without any fear? That little girl still lives inside of you, and she is dying to hit that high G note.

When you focus on the expression of your heart, there is nothing that can be judged because it comes from a place of pure, profound joy.

The Sound of Wind Chimes

There is another method I use to wake up in the moment and reconnect with my inner self. When I hear wind chimes, that's my grandmom saying, *"Hello."*

My grandmom was a little bit of rebel, and that's what I loved about her. She was one of those women who never had a bad thing to say about anyone and always believed in the best in people. She never judged anyone, and that was very important to me because I was going through such a tumultuous time of brutal self-judgment. I understand now that it was all based on the unhealthy behavior that I was involved in, but it didn't make that judgment any easier to handle at the time.

My grandmom always had a way of lightening the mood, of making people laugh. She lived until she was 95 years old and she was as perky and spunky as a 25-year-old. She was the first person to say, *"Let's have Bloody Marys in the morning"* at our family gatherings. We would take her out to exquisite restaurants, and she would take her little airplane bottle full of vodka so that she could order a 7-Up (add her own vodka) and save us money.

She had a special way of bringing fun and lightness to everything and right before she passed away, she gave me a charm bracelet. It was a gold charm bracelet that had faces of little children representing my siblings and cousins on the charms.

She gave me the bracelet because I had mentioned that I loved the sound it made when she wore it. That's when she decided she was going to give it to me. *"I'm not going to wait until I die to give this bracelet to you. I want to be able to give it to you now and see the pleasure on your face when you wear it."* That sound became synonymous with her, and while I don't always have my charm bracelet on, the sound of a wind chime is very similar.

I remember it wasn't long after she passed away that I started connecting her to the sound of wind chimes. When the breeze blows, and I hear a wind chime, it instantly takes me back to thinking about her and how in the midst of the business of life, I can bring lightness and love everywhere I go, just as she did.

ACTION STEP: Role Model Exercise

Who is your role model?

Take a moment to think about someone who has meant something to you. Who is that role model? Write down their name in your Purpose Journal and answer the following questions:

- What did they teach you?
- What essential quality or qualities did you learn from them?
- How were they important in your life?
- What did they mean to you?
- How did they set a good example for you to follow?

Now let's take that a step further.

- How could you be that for someone else?

ACTION STEP: The Role Model Letter

In this exercise, you are going to *hand* write a letter to someone you consider a role model. Tell them how they impacted you, and how you are choosing to share their legacy. If this person is still alive, then drop your letter in the mail. If this person is no longer living, take this opportunity to create a ritual honoring them. Write your letter as though they are still living, read it out loud, and then burn it. You will be amazed at how rewarding this will be.

Reflection of Ourselves in Others

Now let's discover how the qualities we admire in others can be part of the roadmap for us to discover our purpose. When you see positive traits and qualities in someone you respect and admire, it's because you intrinsically know you have similar traits. You can learn so much from people who lift the world. Study them!!

We see our potential in other people because it is often easier to see it in others than it is to see it in ourselves.

Receiving Compliments

Why do women have such a hard time receiving compliments?

It's childhood. It's upbringing. It's this philosophy called, *"Don't be vain, don't be the center of attention, you should be humble."* This culture of deflecting compliments has contributed to the *Purpose Crisis*. We don't see ourselves as other people see us because we can't see the label from inside the bottle. We are not allowing ourselves to recognize our gifts, and we aren't allowing ourselves to receive how others want to honor us. What it comes down to is learning to receive. It's essential for you to wholeheartedly receive a compliment because it's not really about you. It's about the gift that someone is giving you and what you mean to them.

I can't see myself clearly. At times, I view myself through the eyes of what is lacking, because that's been my default. Is this just me? Because of that, I've hired experts and coaches to work with me in all aspects of my life. I've gotten better at recognizing when I'm doing this by becoming aware of this distortion. Now the majority of the time I see myself through my gifts, rather than what I consider to be lacking in me. When we decide to trust a compliment is truly genuine and heartfelt, it deepens the connection with the other person and elevates our understanding of ourselves.

The 5 & 5 Exercise

One on my client exercises is to reach out to five people they respect and admire and request five adjectives describing how that individual perceives them. In the responses, we find patterns and focusing on those common threads reveals areas of giftedness and what makes them uniquely fascinating.

I've also done this exercise for myself. Things that I had not seen before came to light because they were a part of me that I couldn't see for myself. As I read these adjectives, I could see my own patterns. When we see our gifts, we can identify how our strengths tie into our purpose.

ACTION STEP: Complete The 5 & 5 Exercise

Now it's time for you to complete the 5 & 5 Exercise and note the responses and common threads in your Purpose Journal.

Dance Because It Feels Good

We need to get into our bodies more. Our bodies have become a battleground for us. It shows up as a dialogue that goes something like, *"I need to lose weight,"* or *"I need to exercise more,"* or *"I'm so tired."* We're always looking at our self-care as being a chore versus a way of really nurturing ourselves. When we are stuck in our bodies, it impacts the whole of our lives. Many women are in a *Purpose Crisis* because their bodies are completely blocked from communicating with them. We've been trying to figure everything out with our head, and it's no wonder we're cut off from all this other wisdom.

If there's one thing that I know as a healthy, vibrant woman running a successful business, it is imperative for me to focus heavily on my self-care or everything begins to break down. Believe me, I've been there! Part of that is being in tune with my body. When I moved into my apartment, and I had some space and privacy, I started moving more in the morning. It turns out, I love turning music on and getting into my body! Getting into movement and fully experiencing music that touches my soul inspires and energizes me. It actually motivates me to make it a good day.

If I am going to be on sales calls that day, I choose music that gets me grounded and taps into my heart center. If I'm going to be speaking I may listen to "Bad Company" by Five Finger Death Punch because that amps me up. That's my jam.

It's powerful to get into your body, to dance and allow yourself to be free as if nobody is watching you.

I view that as a self-care tool so you can achieve and live your purpose. Living your purpose is all good and well, but it's not always easy. It's hard work, and life has challenges and heartaches. Connecting to your body is all part of the nurture that fuels you forward during the tough times. Movement nurtures the part of us that fuels our purpose and it's physically and mentally good for us, too.

We also know that there's wisdom in the body. The body has understanding, and it's processing emotions all the time. When women's bodies are stuck, they're cut off from a big part of knowing their deeper wisdom.

Doctors and scientists used to think that the brain was the central organ that controlled all of our thinking, feelings, and reactions. Today, neuroscientists have proven that we also have a complex neural network in our abdomen. It's actually like a second brain. This is why we have phrases like, *"trust your gut"* because we instinctually know that we are processing intuition from this part of our body. This research is exciting because it makes sense that we have a second brain in our gut.

What this proves is that the body and mind are more interconnected than we've ever realized. The more you honor your body and allow it to speak to you, the more intelligence you will have to guide your awareness in making clear decisions. By freeing your body, we're accessing more of your intuition, and your innate intelligence. That's where it increases your IQ. Your body can be your friend and ally in finding your purpose.

The more a woman has a positive connection with her body, the more she's able to flow through different times in her life with ease and grace. The more she is in tune to all parts of her intelligence and wisdom, the more fluid she is. And so by honoring your body, you honor your purpose.

4

Purpose Driven Growth

"The purpose of life is undoubtedly to know oneself.
We cannot do it unless we learn to identify
ourselves with all that lives."
Mahatma Gandhi

Why is it important to grow?

If we're not growing, then we're stagnant. Think of it like stagnant water. If you go to a pond that is stagnant, an unhealthy environment grows. When we are flowing, we are growing as individuals. The growth energy is bright, fresh, and clean. We are headed in the direction of our purpose.

As I mentioned earlier, forgiveness is essential to determining your purpose. Forgiveness is the first and most crucial element of growth because when we hold anger and resentment towards ourselves and others, it blocks us from the opportunity to be free and clear. This forgiveness is also crucial in the context of Purpose-Driven Growth so we are going to revisit it.

Time after time when I'm working with clients, issues come up around forgiveness. When we talk about achieving confidence, I often hear women say things like, *"Well I'm not smart enough to do that."* Or *"I don't want to be the center of attention,"* or *"It's not okay for me to draw attention to myself."*

That's what I call, the voice sitting on your shoulder. I always ask the question, *"Whose voice is that?"* Sometimes women will say, *"It's my voice."* And then I'll ask, *"Where did you learn that voice?"* And then there's this aha moment of recognition before they reply, *"That's the way I was raised."*

The idea here is not so we can place blame on anyone, but to recognize where that voice came from to begin with. We can choose to be resentful or compassionate towards that voice or person. Choosing compassion will free you when you look at the voice, or individual, as doing the best they could, given their life experiences. Just as you are, now.

I believe they did love you at some level or their voice wouldn't have such a powerful impact on you. They were doing the best they could, and when you can see that, you can immediately step into a place of forgiveness and letting go. Then you ultimately have to work through the forgiveness layers.

Remember those baby steps to forgiveness that we worked on earlier? Well, now we are going to take it further. Trust me when I tell you that you are ready.

ACTION STEP: Growth-Driven Forgiveness Exercise

This forgiveness exercise is yet another baby step for you to align with your purpose. For one day, stay hyper-focused on every opportunity you have to extend forgiveness.

Let's stay with simple baby steps that are achievable so you'll have success. If someone makes a mistake at work, immediately seek to forgive them. If someone talks to you in a tone of voice you don't like or irritates you in some way, look for opportunities to turn it around. Say to yourself, *"I'm not making this about me. I am going to give grace and forgiveness, whether it's to someone else or to myself."*

In your Purpose Journal write about your day and how choosing forgiveness improved your relationships with others and yourself.

Keep practicing this until forgiveness comes easily.

Learn Something New

"Your brand is the intersection of your purpose, your gifts, your vision, and your values."
- JuliAnn Stitick

Once we identify our purpose and why we are passionate about it, we have to stay current on any information that will foster that purpose.

Learning something new is going to build confidence. The growth can be something that you'd never expect. It could be like me attempting the trapeze. It's crazy for me to say that because I'm afraid of heights! I just made the decision that I was going to face that fear and move beyond it. Once I had made up my mind, I wasn't the least bit nervous as I climbed up the ladder to the platform and stood on the ledge for that first jump.

What does that have to do with our purpose? Well, it's scary to live on purpose. It's a challenge. It's not just, *"Oh here's my purpose and I'm going to walk down this rosy path."* We're going to come up against limiting beliefs, obstacles, and fears. It's when we face those fears head-on that we are going to achieve our desires. More on that later.

If it were easy everybody would do it, right?

ACTION STEP: Ask For Help in One Area of Your Life

We have been programmed to think that we have to do everything ourselves. The truth is that this thinking is very self-centered. NO ONE else can do it all by themselves so why do we think we can? We are here to help each other.

We are here to get through life together and serve one another. When we don't openly receive an offer of assistance from someone, it's the same thing as the unwillingness to accept a compliment. We deny that person the ability to be of service, which is good for them, so in truth, it is selfish to say no.

It's one thing to receive, and it's another thing to ask for help. In those moments where we feel completely overwhelmed or like we can't take another step because there's too much on our plates, it's okay to reach out and say, *"I need help."* I don't know about you, but it feels great when somebody says, *"I could use your help here."* In essence, we are in service to other people when we ask for their support.

People who are on their path to purpose do ask for help. They surround themselves with people that will foster their purpose. And once they find their purpose, they need to keep asking for help to stay on purpose. This is how their purpose will make the most significant impact.

There was a time I was unclear what the next step was for me in my business because there was so much transition going on. I had hired a new marketing team, was transitioning out a personal assistant who had been with me for 6+ years, and I had just hired a CFO. So much change! In the midst of this time, I got clear on my purpose and became hyper-focused about going after it. The right people were showing up. Not only were they the right people for me to work with, but were people that believed in my vision and my purpose. With the energy that each of us brings to the table, it keeps things engaged, exciting, and creative. I know that the people that I've surrounded myself with are in this with me. They are invested and passionate about my purpose because they believe in it.

Find people who believe in your purpose.

5

Purpose-Fueling Environment

"If there were no night, we would not appreciate the day, nor could we see the stars and the vastness of the heavens. We must partake of the bitter with the sweet. There is a divine purpose in the adversities we encounter every day. They prepare, they purge, they purify, and thus they bless."
James E. Faust

For us to achieve our purpose in life, we have to create environments that nurture it. If we are living in an environment that is chaotic or cluttered or tumultuous, it makes it difficult for us to stay on target. A healthy environment, whether it be external or internal, is crucial in fostering the birth of your purpose.

Internal Environment

Let's start with your internal environment. Our internal environment is our mindset and how we choose to look at the world. It's what we are doing to nurture our spirituality and our souls.

What are we doing to cultivate our minds? When I think about the inner environment, I immediately think about my decision not to watch or read the news. I filter what goes into my intimate atmosphere. It's just like that saying, *"garbage in, garbage out."* I truly believe that what goes in is bound to manifest itself in my mindset and behavior.

It's essential to surround yourself with people who are confident, honest, and who will lift you up. You want to align yourself with others who will do what they say they're going to do, and who look at the world as being much more significant than what they can grasp. That's a way of filtering your internal environment. You are protecting your mind and heart from people who bring negativity into your awareness.

The spiritual work that happens inside of you is about connecting with whatever your higher power is. It doesn't matter what your belief system is as long as you have something bigger than yourself that you can connect to.

The Purpose Filter

"Thoughts are to a man, what water is to the fish."
- Buddha

Whatever you allow into your inner environment affects your ability to be on track with your purpose. If negative thinking and fear surround you, whether it's coming from the media, or news, or television or movies, then that's going to impact your inner environment. Just like the fish that's swimming in a toxic pool, you're going to become part of that toxic environment.

You are your own filter and you make the choices. You need to take responsibility for your inner environment and turn your filter on full blast. I call it The Purpose Filter. It's your commitment to yourself to take responsibility for your choice of people around you, the books you read, the movies you watch, etc.

Remember to go back to that original question we asked in the beginning, *"What does this have to do with the intention of my soul?"* In every decision that we make, this question needs to be at the forefront of your mind.

The Curse of Judgment

I do not believe in judging other people. I value non-judgment very highly. Just because I have a belief or opinion about something, it doesn't mean that everyone else has to have that same belief. It's not my responsibility to change people's minds about their beliefs. It is above my pay grade to judge what somebody else does or what they believe. It is none of my business.

Judgment has many negative implications. First of all, when you're judging, you're putting all of your energy out on somebody else and you are wasting that precious life energy.

It drains you, and you don't have the focus on your purpose. You need all of your energies to be on caring for yourself so you can serve others — your health, your body, your thinking, et cetera. The judgment of others is a never-ending suction of your precious energy.

But it doesn't stop there. In psychology, there's this thing called projection. It turns out that the things you are judging about other people, are the things you are denying or avoiding about yourself. Otherwise, you wouldn't even care about what you consider these shortcomings unless you were identifying with some part of yourself.

The third negative impact of judgment is that you are hurting people. If they feel you are judging them, then you are not a light to the world. You're not honoring their soul and their path.

This is powerful. When we are judging other people, we are in an ego state because we feel that we know what's better for them than they do. (Now, it's different when you're talking about raising children. Obviously, you need to guide your children to avoid them making mistakes.) What I'm referring to is people judging other people for their political beliefs, religion, how they choose to live their life, spend their money, or who they choose to love.

In this internal environment, we want to stay focused on our purpose and eliminate judgment... completely. That includes judgment of yourself! As I mentioned earlier, when you are concerned that others are judging you it's really because you are judging yourself!

When you can clear out self-judgment, and stop judging other people, you're not concerned with other's opinions of you. It's a vibration that is removed from your life forever, and it will never show up again.

Even if other people *are* judging you, when you get clear on your purpose, you don't care anymore. It's so liberating to feel this to the core of your being, *"I'm on my path, and if you don't agree with my way, God bless you."*

When a person is free of judgment, they shine. They have a different aura about them. They're not judging themselves, they're not judging others. When you meet them, you have the distinct honor of experiencing their soul.

The Outer Environment

Now let's focus on your living environment. What is it like when you walk into your home?

Now I understand there are some things, depending on your situation, that you have control over and some things you don't. We want to start where you can and begin to look at your home as a womb. It is a place of safety, calm, peace, and security from the outside world. Your home is a place where you can recharge and fuel your purpose.

When you walk into my home, it feels like you're walking into a spa. The colors are soft, and it's cozy. The textures are rich and soft. Essential oils are diffusing 24/7. The lighting is pleasant and I've got music playing. It's music that lifts me or calms me depending on the time of day.

As I prepare to travel, I make sure my place is tidy and my auto-timer is set so that shortly before I return my diffuser goes on and starts essential oils wafting through my home.

If I'm going to be getting back in the evening, I will turn down my bed, like turndown service at a hotel. I fold my pajamas and put them on my bed while my slippers wait at the ready. By creating an environment that is free of clutter and relaxing, I can let go, be free, unwind and get quality sleep.

Taking care of our environment is essential to remove the *Purpose Crisis* from our life. For us to honestly know and understand the depth of our purpose, we need a place for respite. We need a place to let down our guard to discover what is really underneath. To do that, we have to surround ourselves with an environment that nurtures us. Then we can open ourselves up to reveal and relax into our purpose.

Does your environment nurture you? What are some changes you can make today that will elevate your environment?

Relation-Fueling Environment

We've covered the purpose-fueling environment. We've explored the inner environment and the outer environment, and now we need to explore the relational environment.

What do I mean when I say relational environment?

The relational environment is all about the health of the relationships in your life that are closest to you. Only when we have clear connections with people can we genuinely fuel our purpose.

Life can be messy, and everyone is living their life the best way they know how to based on their experiences.

The first thing we have to address is that we don't have control over every part of our relationships. We only have control over our side of the street. The tricky part is knowing what we do and don't have control over.

It seems like it should be so easy to say, *"This is my responsibility, and this is yours,"* but so often when we want to be helpful, and we care about someone else, it's easy to step into what doesn't belong to us. We try to control them without being aware that we are doing so.

I make it my goal to know that my contribution to each relationship is clean and bright. Does that mean that I don't ever have issues with other people? No, that's not what that means. As humans, we bump into each other in life. It's certainly not because we plan to hurt someone's feelings, but we're humans, and we all make mistakes.

If we get triggered by another person, we need to determine, *"Is this an opportunity to give grace?"* Let's say an acquaintance said the wrong thing or used the wrong tone of voice. We can take that personally if we choose to, but we can also choose to understand that this person might be having a bad day. It's our choice to say, *"I'm not going to make it about me."*

That's what we are talking about when we say Relational Environment. A clean environment is in alignment with my message about creating the space to allow free-flowing thoughts and personal expression.

I've seen that women can become obsessive about trying to control other people. Or if something is off in a relationship, they can loop on it over and over again. Instead of being able to focus on the responsibility they have in their relationships, they are spending time and energy in drama.

Let's make our intention to keep our relationships clean. When a challenge or conflict arises ask yourself, *"What can I own about this?"* Use that knowledge to springboard into your personal awareness for purpose-fueling growth. Then, let things go when you realize that it's not yours to own.

If I have a hiccup in a relationship, my default is always to ask myself, *"How do I have a responsibility in this?"* I have to look at myself, first and foremost. I have to see how I have acted or responded, and ask myself, *"Was I responding out of love and selflessness, or was I being reactive and making it about me? Was I too sensitive?"* When I can take responsibility for how I am, it becomes much easier for me to let go of someone else's actions.

Let me give you an example. There's a story I heard about two gentlemen who were walking in downtown New York City. They approached a newsstand, and the newsy was rude to them. One of the gentlemen was very kind to him in return. The other gentleman said, *"I cannot believe you were so nice to that guy. He was terrible to you!"* Then the first gentleman said, *"I'm not going to let how other people treat me dictate how I act towards them."*

We must take responsibility for our own actions. Not trying to lay the blame, but asking, *"What could I have done differently? And Is there something that I need to apologize for?"* If that's the case, then apologize right away so you can be clean about it. Now comes the tough part... apologize without the expectation of how that other person is going to receive it.

When I can lay my head down on my pillow at night and know that I acted out of love and ownership of who I am and what my actions are, I sleep soundly because I'm not spinning my wheels about why that other person may have wronged me or hurt my feelings. I'm able to let it go.

If they decide to apologize, great. I will receive that and accept their apology willingly. If the person does not apologize, then I have an understanding that it is their journey, not mine. The other person's reaction is not my responsibility. I can let go of that. If there is something that feels unresolved, I know if I continue to stay in love and accountability to myself, everything will end up working out in the long run.

I don't know what the outcome is going to be every time, but I do know that it always ends up working out. I have to allow other people their process. Their process is not necessarily going to be in my timing, but it's perfect in God's timing. For me to think that I am going to make them act a certain way is delusional and arrogant.

When a woman is on purpose, she has a clear understanding of which relationships in her life are healthy and which are not.

A former coach assigned an exercise, that at first, I thought was odd. On a piece of paper, she had me draw 10 columns. She asked me to head each of the columns with a trait or value I admire and want in the people I surround myself with. Then, she had me list the 5 people I spent the most time with down the far-left column.

Next, she had me go across and check off all of traits/values each person had. What was really interesting was that patterns became very, very clear. What this exercise did was help me identify that two of the people I was spending considerable time with were not on target in fueling my purpose. They were fun and adventurous, but they brought drama consistently and were not respecting me.

Not that they were terrible people. There isn't any judgment here. It's merely that I am the one who decides what my relational environments are going to be like and you can too.

ACTION STEP: Top 10 Qualities Exercise

Go through this exact same exercise that I just described. In your Purpose Journal, list across the top of the page ten qualities that you value in others.

Down the left column, list the five people with whom you spend the most time. Put a checkmark next to each quality that this person demonstrates. Repeat for each person.

Did you notice any patterns? What are the patterns? What does this tell you about the relationships that you are cultivating in your life? Are any of these people missing the qualities that matter most to you? How can you be more mindful of looking for these qualities as you form new relationships? How can you find people who carry these qualities? Write down your answers to these questions in your Purpose Journal.

Your Purpose Compass

You know what's coming to me? A visual of a purpose compass.

This compass points to your true north. When you're aligned with your purpose, you are moving towards your true north. When you have a purpose compass, it points you in the direction of your true self. As you travel through life, your relationships may pull you away from that true north, but you're aware of it. You feel it, and you pause, *"Whoa, this doesn't align with my purpose,"* and you're able to recalibrate.

When your relationships are feeding your purpose, it's like the wind is at your back and pushing you forward without any friction. Your relationships are supporting you, making your purpose clearer and more powerful every day.

This all feeds into the importance of finding the right community and surrounding yourself with people who are supportive of your purpose. The more support you have, the more directly you move towards your true north. The easier it will be to stay on your purpose.

Another exercise I assign my clients is The Values Exercise. From an extensive list of values, I ask them to identify their top 5. Yep, only 5. First, they begin by choosing 20. Then we narrow it to 10, and then narrow it down again to 5.

Knowing your top 5 values creates clarity in moving towards your purpose. As you continue to look at your relational environment, you'll further ask, *"Does this person value the same things I do? Do they value my purpose?"*

Why is it important to surround yourself with people who value your purpose?

When you have a purpose, it's not always easy. Roadblocks can show up in the form of health issues, relational challenges and financial struggles, to name a few.

As we face these obstacles and challenges, it's essential that we have people in our circle who are going to walk the path and travel the journey with us. They won't be looking down on us or belittling our purpose. They won't put negative energy around the actions we're taking.

When you have a purpose you're stepping into the place of being a great visionary. Being a visionary is terrifying to some people because of their fear of being seen. When you step into that space of being a visionary, you've got to make sure that you are surrounding yourself with people who are going to help nurture that vision.

It's not to say that they won't question you or even call you out on some things. They may be asking you some of the hard questions, and that's important. As long as they're doing this from a place of support, their actions are going to foster your vision. It's not about surrounding yourself with "yes" people either. It's about surrounding yourself with people whom you respect and admire. You will know it when you look at these people and think to yourself, *"I admire that person and desire those qualities for myself, too."*

Also, surround yourself with people that are smarter than you. I've always said, *"I never, ever want to be at the head of the class."* This keeps your ego in check and ensures you are developing relationships that keep you in integrity with your purpose.

6

Purpose Mindset

"You become what you believe."
Oprah Winfrey

Knowing your purpose is a crucial step in radiating success in your life. It's the fuel inside that shows through the twinkle in your eyes and the glow in your presence. Yep.

A purpose is a reason for which something is done, created or exists. The point here is to determine the reason you were created. Yes, it's that simple and complex at the same time.

Ok, dig deep into your heart now. Stop. Close your eyes and take a deep, long breath. Now visualize your heart expanding bigger and bolder. Take a deep breath. Hold it. Let it out. As you continue to breathe, relax your shoulders. Smile at your heart and read on.

Think of a time in your life when you accomplished something significant. Something that tapped into your passion and excited you. Something you worked hard to achieve. Likely you recognize that it took strength, skills, and energy that surprised even you. You were driven, laser-focused, and felt on fire! Your purpose was aligned like a concentrated beam of sunlight, although you may not have known that you were on purpose at the time.

You may be saying, *"I still don't know what my purpose is."* If so, think BIG. The sky is the limit. Here's what I mean. When asked what her purpose was, my client Susan said, *"My purpose is to be a good mother."* Let's dig a little deeper and broader than that.

Your purpose is where your values, strengths, and desires intersect. Let me demonstrate that using Susan's scenario.

Susan's Values: Family, Fun, Love, Creativity, Generosity

Susan's Strengths: Creative, Innovative, Leadership, Illustration, Organization, Event Planning

Susan's Desires: To improve the lives of others using fun and creativity.

It wasn't until Susan had intersected the trio of Values, Strengths, and Desires in the exercise above that she began to understand what her more significant purpose was. You see, Susan had always dreamed of opening a local non-profit center to help children learn through the arts. Now, she runs that non-profit with her children. AMAZING! Bravo Susan. Can you see how her values, strengths and desires intersected?

Knowing your purpose helps you identify the basis for your growth mindset. It gives you a grounding, a golden thread, a touch point for making sure your mindset and ultimately your actions will help you achieve your reason for being created.

Clarity of purpose is a powerful step in living a life that excites you. It's also the juice that gives you the stamina to stick out the hard times. Now it's time to take a few moments to complete this exercise for yourself.

ACTION STEP: The Purpose Trinity

In your Purpose Journal identify your Values, Strengths and Desires. Now dig deep and ask yourself, "What do I really want to do with those gifts?"

Once you have more clarity, take some time to write about your purpose's vision. For Susan, it was describing what the center would look like, the smiles on the children's faces as they learned a new concept, the pride in the parents' eyes as they watched their child achieve new heights.

Don't hold back, either. When we begin to dream big, those voices that sit on our shoulders pop their heads up and say things like, *"It will cost too much money." "It would be too overwhelming, and I wouldn't have the time." "My family will never truly support my decisions."* Lovingly recognize those voices likely belong to someone in your past who unknowingly influenced you based on their own hang-ups and history. Now it's time to visualize brushing those voices off your shoulder and standing firmly in the desire you have to contribute in a more significant way.

Remember, you are here for an important reason as unique as your fingerprints. Even if you do not honestly believe in yourself yet, I believe in you. I believe in the hope you bring to the world. You are special. You are beautiful. You matter.

Be Present

What does it mean to be present? It means fully experiencing all of your senses in the current moment. You are so aware of your surroundings in all aspects that your mind doesn't have the space to think about past or future events. Sounds nice, doesn't it?

Children are born being genuinely present, and it's socialization that pulls them away from being entirely in the moment.

During my research, I found some children's books about being present, taking the time for mindfulness, actively listening, and one of my favorites, the importance of silence. Bravo to our children's authors and the impact they are making on a new generation of more enlightened and happier children.

One of those books is called *The Listening Walk* by Paul Showers. This book is an introduction to careful listening. It shows us how a simple walk can turn into a lesson in mindfulness. As the little girl in the story focuses on her walking trail, she is able to hear, see, smell, and experience things she otherwise would not. At the end of the story, we are invited to take a listening walk. Ok, I think I will!

The reason this resonated with me was because I practice active listening to stay present. Each day as I walk Lily around town or at the local park, I keep my head up and my cell phone tucked away safely in my pocket. I look at the beautiful mountains against the blue sky with white puffy clouds. I look into the eyes of the homeless man or his dog. I look for opportunities to interact with my fellow humans. I smile warmly at as many people as I can. You'd chuckle at how many of those people are uncomfortable with that connection. That's ok, it still touches them in the way they are able to receive on that day.

I marvel at Lily sniffing the plants and watching her little tail rapidly motoring back and forth as she greets new people. I listen to the mix of birds, the breeze in the trees, and a distant wind chime tinkling (Hi, Grandmom!). And then there are the smells like the melaleuca tree or jasmine!

I'm mindful of how my body is feeling, too. As I walk, am I holding my body in a posture that is healthy to my core strength? Am I tensed and needing to drop my shoulders? Do I need to drink some water (always)? Is it time to fuel myself with a handful of pecans or string cheese?

It's not always easy to stay present. I lose that focus at times when I'm working. I often catch myself lost in a distraction. One minute I'm answering an email, and then I glance at something on my desk. That takes me off on a complete mental journey away from my keyboard to filling out bank forms. Huh, how did I get here?

Perfection is not the goal. The goal is to be making progress. By giving myself grace when I do get caught up in the distraction of my mind, I find humor in it.

One of my late mentors, Don, would ask this question every time I saw him, *"JuliAnn, are you being gentle with yourself?"* There were sometimes I rolled my eyes and said, *"Yeah, right!"* We would chuckle, and he would remind me that I am deserving of kindness.

Now, each time I find myself interacting with the committee that lives in my head or the multitude of items on my to-do list, I remember Don's words and gently shift my mind back to the task at hand.

Being present is also a GREAT remedy for anxiety. When I find myself tensed, agitated, or overwhelmed I remind myself to stand right where I am, take in my current surroundings, and do what I can to make those surroundings a kind and loving place. When I transport my mind to the present and stay in the now, my body actually calms down.

Being present makes you more charismatic, too! If you meet someone at a networking event and their eyes are scanning the room behind you, do you feel unique and valuable? No way. Is this individual charming or magnetic? Probably not. Their mind is apparently in another place. Possibly they are trying to find someone "more important" than you. They are not truly listening to you or focusing on your conversation. Do you think you'll want to connect with them again? Doubtful.

If you meet someone who makes you feel like you're the only person in the room, you will definitely find them likable and interesting. Let's take that a step further. What if their cell phone rings and they do not check it? That is a valuable gift being handed to you — their time and attention.

Charismatic people are influential because they connect with people in a meaningful way. It's so rare to receive this kind of attention, and the ability to stay fully present makes a huge impression. One of the most extensive studies on charisma found that charisma is more about the practice of being fully present than it is an innate gift. The study pointed out six elements of a charismatic person:

1. Empathy: the ability to understand how a person is feeling by seeing things through their eyes.
2. Good Listening Skills: paying close attention to what people are communicating to you both verbally and nonverbally.
3. Eye contact: maintaining the gaze of another.
4. Enthusiasm: the ability to encourage and uplift another through your actions or words.
5. Self-confidence: the ability to be yourself without worrying about what other people think. Many people are so busy worrying about how they look that they end up coming across as self-absorbed

or even inauthentic. Their focus is on themselves rather than the person they are talking to. When you are fully present, you are focused on others rather than on yourself. As a lovely result, you naturally come across as confident, composed and genuine.

6. Skillful speaking: the ability to connect deeply with others.

As you can see, being present has a multitude of benefits for yourself and others.

ACTION STEP: Listening Walk Exercise

Take 5 minutes today to go on your own listening walk where you can be in nature. If you don't live in or near natural wilderness, find a beautiful local park. Yes, you can go for longer than 5 minutes if you'd like, but the key here is go for at least 5 minutes. My hope is that you will enjoy it so much, you will want to do it for longer.

- Where did you take your listening walk?
- Describe what you heard
- Describe what you saw
- Describe what you smelled
- Describe how your body felt
- Described how it made you feel

Commit to taking a 5-minute listening walk today. Tomorrow, make that commitment again. The next day, commit again. The key here is to take things one day at a time. Eventually, the days add up and you will have achieved your goal of making this a habit.

Pep Talk: My dear sister, you are worth so much. You are worth living a life you are proud to call your own. You're worth living a life where you are calm, peaceful, happy and present. You may be thinking, *"I would love to live a life of calm, peace, being happy and present, but you don't know my circumstances."* You are right; I don't know your circumstances. Although the details of our lives are different, we are all the same. We all have worth. You are worth having a mindset that is clear, focused, and intentional. From the bottom of my heart, I want you to know how very special you are. You were put here for a reason only you can achieve. Carry your head high today, smile at the people you meet, and remember there is such good inside of you so let it show.

In a nutshell, being present will improve your self-esteem, make you calmer, healthier, a better friend, spouse, partner, parent, and more successful in every area of your life. You will live a more productive, fuller, and happier life.

Now that you have made the decision to be present, you will always know your purpose when you are living in the present moment.... okay maybe it's not quite that simple and it's going to take some time and practice. We are going to need more exercises to make this "staying present" mindset a habit.

ACTION STEP: Becoming Your Own Present

There are many ways of strengthening this "staying present" muscle. Everyone has a unique way of coming into the present, and it is not always the same. It's important to discover your own way of becoming present that you can go to again and again. I like to think of this as "becoming your own present".

- In your Purpose Journal name 3 examples from the past week when you were not staying present?

- What are 3 ways you can become present?

Purpose Challenge: For 24 hours, be keenly mindful of staying in the now. Check in at the end of that 24 hours and then name 3 ways staying present improved your day? Write about this in your Purpose Journal.

Here are 20 of my favorite ways of getting into the present moment:

1. Feel the sun on your skin
2. Appreciate who you're with
3. Cuddle with your dog
4. Hug a loved one
5. Wait patiently in line
6. Notice your breath coming in and out of your body
7. Listen carefully when other people are speaking
8. Notice when someone needs help and take the time to help
9. Be grateful for your family and friends by telling them you appreciate them
10. Savor each bite of your food
11. Listen to the sound of the rain
12. Feel the sand, soil, or grass between your toes
13. Taste the ocean's salty spray
14. Close your eyes and be still
15. Take a deep breath and lengthen your spine
16. Close your eyes and let your shoulders relax
17. Slowly drink a glass of water
18. Listen intently to the lyrics of songs
19. Smile as you pass someone on the street
20. Study the subtle shades of green on a leaf

We've discussed the importance of deciding to have a great mindset. We've further explored our purpose. We've addressed the importance of being in the moment and staying present. Now, it's time to have a quality day.

In the following chapters, I will be using examples and stories to teach the elements of having a quality day. It's time to learn how you can change the course of your day through simple actions.

Mindset

Mindset is everything. In a purpose mindset, it's really about knowing that your abilities can be grown and stretched through hard work and dedication to your soul's mission. It's a view that creates a passion for learning and the resilience needed for that purpose.

I see mindset as being the foundation for my reality. It's the way I choose to think and look at things that enter my mind. The ideas and beliefs of what I set in my mind will ultimately unfold. In other words, what I think and believe and say, will happen.

Some time ago, my husband and I were shopping for patio furniture. Let's just say we were having a real difference of opinion and some hot buttons were being pressed for both of us. We left the store and were driving home, but we were not in a happy place. We were going to go back home and have some space, but I turned to him and said, *"We have the ability right now to change today. We can say, that didn't go so well. What can we do now to shift the day? We can have a nice day together so that we're not going to go home and go our separate ways and feel bad. Let's change things."*

He looked at me, and he said, *"Okay, let's do it."* We ended up going out to lunch, and while we were walking from our car to the restaurant, we came

upon a man who was creating floral arrangements out of the back of his old, beat up truck. We engaged him in conversation, and he told us he was working two jobs to make ends meet. I complimented him on his arrangement, *"These flowers are so beautiful."* In broken English he replied, *"It is my job to make people happy."*

That was his purpose — making others happy through the beauty of flowers. When we were getting ready to leave, he reached into the back of the truck and pulled out a bouquet of purple and white lilacs and presented them to me.

It shifted our day. It changed how Joe and I interacted the rest of the day. Then we decided to brave one more patio furniture store and we ended up finding the perfect patio set! We walked out of the store laughing, and I said to Joe, *"Wow, that guy that sold us the furniture is probably going to think that we are the most agreeable couple."* We came in there on purpose, and we knew what we wanted. We worked together as a team.

The day was a success, but it was only a success because we stopped and made a decision to change our mindset for the day. It changed the outcome to be sure.

Challenge Your Perspective

Many people believe that their intelligence and their strengths are fixed traits in them. They measure their gifts instead of developing them. They think, *"This is the way that I was born, and this is just the way I am."*

What that means is that they have an established way of thinking. The definition of established is *"having been in existence for a long time and therefore recognized and generally accepted."* It's also an attitude or a settled way of thinking or feeling about someone or something. I think that's where the term mind*set* comes from—the mind is set on a way of thinking.

At times it's tough to shift our mindset because it has been set for some time, and it's something we feel like is part of us. It's easy to get stuck because we're on autopilot. When we know that we can change our mindset, the whole world of possibility opens up for us.

This is what I call The Mindset Triad:

1. Make a Decision
2. Know Your Purpose
3. Be Present

When you follow these steps, you will be able to see the best perspective for you in each and every moment. It may change as you continue to grow and align with your inner Purpose Compass. That is a sign that you are moving closer to your true north.

The Mindset Triad

The Mindset Triad is three steps to changing your mindset. First, you have to decide to change your mindset.

Here's a quick story to give you an example of what I mean. My dad was being wheeled into the surgical center for his colonoscopy. He had begrudgingly endured the prior day's prep of drinking the disgusting liquid and spending an inordinate amount of time in the bathroom. He'd been struggling with many health issues, and this was just one of many tests and procedures that he had to endure for the immediate future.

He was chatting up his nurse as she guided his gurney into the treatment room and prepped him for the not-so-pleasant procedure. She assured him he could check this test off the list shortly. He responded by saying something that surprised her: *"Well, it's not so bad. Think of it this way. I've entirely detoxed my body, and that's good, isn't it?"*

That had not been his tune the previous day as he complained to my mom about how inconvenient and uncomfortable the whole process was. She patiently and consistently responded that it was for his good. My mom kept reminding him he could choose to look at the situation as a positive. He was cleansing his body and narrowing down the cause of his health issues. Here he was sharing her exact words with the nurse. My mom would never have believed after all these years that her positive mindset could change his!

My mother enjoyed how upbeat he was as they drove home that rainy Wednesday afternoon. He went on to tell her that he had just decided to look at it from the bright side as if it was all his idea. It had gone much smoother than he could have anticipated based on his past experiences. He had unknowingly been lured into choosing the bright side.

We all have the power of choice. We can decide how to act in every situation. Who we become is a product of the decisions that we've made, from the types of people we surround ourselves with, and the way we spend our time each day. What we don't realize is that we have the power to decide exactly how to feel about a situation, too.

My Spinal Surgery Story

I was scheduled for spine surgery the fall of 2017. It was a big decision, and I had heard some horror stories from friends and family about why I should not have the procedure.

Had I tried acupuncture? Yes.

Had I done physical therapy? Yep.

Was I exercising in a way that was helping to strengthen the weak areas? Mm-hmm.

Did I believe my back could stop hurting? Yes.

Was I taking all the right supplements? Heavens, yes.

Was I wearing shoes that were aggravating the pain? No.

Was I sitting too much? No. I had purchased a motorized desk, so I could stand or sit as necessary.

It was a very stressful and physically painful time. I remember the August day clearly when I took a deep breath, picked up the phone to call the surgeon's office, and scheduled the surgery. As I hung up, I had an immediate sense of peace about the whole thing. Right then and there, I made the decision I was going to heal quickly and successfully, so I put my plan into action.

One: Schedule an out-of-town speaking engagement five weeks after my surgery. Yep. Daunting, but what the heck? I'm a risk taker.

Two: Continue to exercise and keep my core strong so that I could recover quickly.

Three: Eat healthily and be consistent with my supplements so I could strengthen my immune system.

Four: Pray and meditate regularly with a focus on rest and healing.

Five: Commit to stop using pain medication as early on in my recovery as possible. I didn't want to mask my pain so I could be fully aware of my body and treat it accordingly.

Six: Follow the doctor's recovery directions to a T.

Seven: Gently push my body every day. I began using a walker and making it 100 feet. The next day, I went to 120. The following day, I ditched the walker and started to make it on my own. A few days later, I did a flight of stairs.

Within five weeks, I was boarding a plane to Wichita for that speaking engagement.

I vividly remember the trip. I flew all day Wednesday, spoke Thursday, and woke up Friday morning for another full day of travel. We landed in LA, and as I made my way to the street to meet my ride, I had the sudden realization that my back didn't hurt. What a wonderful moment!

People were shocked to see how quickly I was back up on my feet enjoying life, pain-free, may I add. I had chosen to heal successfully, and I did. I had made a choice.

You may be saying, *"That's easy for you. You healed quickly."* I will tell you that if there had been any complications, I would have handled them like the champion my grandmom and mom taught me to be. I will always choose to be energetic, dedicated, and not willing to stay in a place of self-pity for long, if at all.

Just like my dad's positive attitude about his colonoscopy or my opinion about my spine surgery, once you've decided to improve your mindset, there are countless ways you can build and foster the type of life you see in your vision.

The second step in The Mindset Triad is knowing your purpose. Understanding your purpose is a crucial step in radiating success in your life.

Knowing your purpose is the second piece in helping you identify the basis for your mindset. Clarity of purpose is a powerful step in living a life that excites you. It's also the touchstone that gives you the stamina to stick out the hard times.

The third piece in The Mindset Triad is being present. I talked about what it means to be present. Scientifically speaking, present-moment awareness involves monitoring and attending to current experience rather than predicting future events or dwelling on the past.

Yes, I know we just covered this in detail, but it is worth repeating until it becomes who you are and not just a concept.

Practice The Mindset Triad as often as necessary until it becomes as natural as breathing. It can happen! You will be fueling your purpose with precious, positive energy.

The Importance of Gratitude

Gratitude is much easier for some people while others really have to work at it. Sure, some people are just wired to be grateful and optimistic, but it is also a learned skill.

Gratitude is a decision to look at life from a place of abundance rather than focusing on what is lacking. There's that "decision" word again. I'm sure you are starting to notice the theme by now.

One of my favorite quotes is, *"The feelings follow the actions."* We typically want to feel like doing something before we do it. There are days I don't feel like getting out of my warm bed, putting my workout clothes on, and going to the gym. You may relate to that. Here's what I know about this lack of motivation — when I get up and start moving, the feelings follow.

We can choose gratitude even if we begin with resistance! Again, it's making a decision that you're going to look at life from a place of gratitude. The importance of living in gratitude is how we choose to live a positive experience. Sometimes, especially when I'm going through a difficult time, it's hard to focus on the little things (that are not so little) like having a warm, clean bed to sleep in every night. I have food to eat every day. I have a body that works. Even with its occasional aches and pains, it still works. I'm grateful that I can see, smell, hear, feel, taste and touch.

What things can you be grateful for?

It's the same thing in our relationships. If we decide that we want to dwell on what we're thankful for in a person, that's what's going to grow. You nurture in that relationship what you're grateful for. What we focus on expands, and when we can look at life from a place of gratitude, we then begin to see growth from a place of appreciation.

Gratitude lists are powerful. One of the things I do each day is write down five things I'm grateful for about myself. I'm empathetic, witty, make a mean apple pie, have an infectious laugh, and can be very persistent. Being thankful for the things I appreciate about myself helps build the value I see in myself and builds up my self-worth. That's part of my self-care routine in the morning. (More on that in a bit.)

When I am building my worth internally and powerfully, I am able to shift my attitude when I'm sitting in traffic, for instance. I can be grateful I have a car that works, gasoline to fuel it, and spa music I can listen to while I'm navigating the gridlock.

ACTION STEP: Gratitude List

In your Purpose Journal create an ongoing list of the things you are grateful for about yourself.

Gratitude has been proven to calm the nervous system. When you can shift into gratitude, you take deeper breaths. You're able to think clearer. It also

helps us to make decisions from a place of strength rather than a place of weakness.

I am grateful for you and your purpose.

7

Purpose-Driven Self Care

"The purpose of our lives is to be happy."
- Dalai Lama

When you are unorganized, you will be wasting all your precious time and energy on things that don't matter. I'm known as the "Queen of the Checklists" because I see that my life is so much more productive when I'm organized. Those checklists help keep this creative creature on target!

I've shared these checklists with my clients over the years, and I've even written an entire book about preparing for a special event like a conference or special event. The book is called *Step Into Your Power* and you can get a free copy of that book by going here to www.GetYourPowerBook.com

We are going to go through my personal self-care routines and rituals. These are methods that have taken me years to develop, and I continue to fine tune them. I find the more I systemize my life, the more space I feel in my mind to explore the most critical conversations like staying in alignment with my purpose. Let's get you there too.

Weekly Prep Day

Many women live their lives helter-skelter, without any planning or preparation. That used to be me. All the extras in your life are pushed aside until it becomes this massive to-do list that seems overwhelming. All of these little things add up over time and cause mental and emotional stress.

I love having one day a week where I focus 100% of my energy on taking care of the busy-work in my life. These are tasks that don't really add much value to my bottom line, but they have to get done. When I knock it out in one day, I have the rest of the week to care for myself, my family, and my business.

As a creative person, it's essential for me to block out my time because it gets difficult for me to effectively move back and forth between the regions of my brain. It also takes a tremendous amount of mental energy to jump from my heart (like when I'm coaching clients) and into my head (to handle financial matters) and then back down into my heart. If I want to be effective at what I'm doing with my time, I have to give myself that block of time where I can make it all happen at once.

This is why I created my Weekly Prep Day. If I need to file insurance claims, go to the DMV, take Lily to the vet, pay bills, or grocery shop — this is the day it all gets done. The rest of the week, I am entirely focused on business development, meeting with clients, and networking to grow my business. Knowing all my "to do's" have been taken care of, gives me the head space to focus on the bigger picture. In other words, it gives me the freedom to seek out my purpose.

Another thing I do on my Weekly Prep Day is I pull out my calendar and look at the week ahead. *"What do I need for the rest of this week?"*

Let's say I'm going to a networking event on Friday. For that event, I think about all the things I'm going to need to make the best impression. What items do I need to take with me? I choose a handbag or tote based on how much space I need and pack it. Then I save the event address in my navigation app. I've chosen an outfit that makes me feel fabulous. I've entirely prepared myself on my Weekly Prep Day, so it's simple to grab my bag Friday morning and head out the door knowing I am fully prepared!

I go into my entire pre-event prep system in my book, *Step Into Your Power*. I'm so passionate about being prepared and organized, I wrote a whole separate book for it! Make sure you get your copy at www.GetYourPowerBook.com

Morning Ritual

When you are a woman with a purpose, it's essential to create rituals in your life to make sure you continue to stay on this path. It is so easy to get distracted or go back to sleep, but this is one of the factors that caused the *Purpose Crisis* to begin with.

The morning time is a sacred time to create a ritual where you clear your mind and align your body, heart, and soul with the intention of your purpose.

There is a clear difference between women who have this morning ritual and those who do not. Early morning time is a time when you do not have the challenges of the day stressing you out or pulling you away from your focus. When you create a ritual for yourself in the morning, the rest of your day will flow with more ease and grace.

ACTION STEP: Set Your Morning Ritual

As you read through this section create your ritual in your Purpose Journal.

Creating a ritual and finding the time to execute it, may seem hard at first, but soon you will begin to crave this alone time you are setting aside for yourself in the morning.

If possible, give yourself a minimum of 90 minutes (I give myself 2 hours) to complete your morning ritual. That may seem like a lot of time to dedicate to yourself, but believe me, you'll be glad you did. If your family life or work schedule prohibits you from taking this time in the morning, find a way to plug these rituals into your life in a way that works for YOU.

When you discover how much more energy, peace, and clarity you find from this morning ritual, you will see it is more valuable than anything else you can do for yourself. You will eventually schedule your sleeping to go to bed earlier because you will want to wake up with ease. In the beginning, you may have to force yourself out of bed, but this won't be for long.

When you wake up in the morning, do NOT check your phone, your social media, or your email or, God forbid, turn on the news. There's ample research on the effects of technology on our brain waves, and we need to channel our first moments of waking to be used in positive ways. Technology and the agenda of others will create stress in your brain waves. You want to use this time as a set point for your brain waves to create a sense of well-being and peacefulness throughout the day.

I have developed an 8 Step Morning Ritual, and it has literally changed my life. I have more clarity, look and feel better and can manage the stressors that come up in my daily life.

Step 1: Meditate

Make your favorite morning beverage. It can be coffee, tea, or warm water with lemon to hydrate you. You don't want to fall asleep while you are meditating, so be sure you are alert (or at lease semi-alert) before you sit in your meditation posture.

Once you are hydrated and you've taken care of your biological needs, find a place in your home where you can rest comfortably without dozing off to sleep again. Your bed is associated with sleep, and so it's best to sit in either a comfortable chair or on a cushion that you can set on the floor.

With your spine straight, fold your hands in your lap or place them on your knees. Begin to breathe deeply into your abdomen, filling up your lungs with air. It's important to infuse our bodies with oxygen when we first wake up because it is the #1 nutrient for every cell of our bodies.

As you are breathing deeply and smoothly, you may find your mind is already starting to race with the day's agenda and to-do list. This is your mental training. Simply tell your brain to return to your breath. Your to-do list will be there when you get to it. I promise.

This is your time to release any heavy, toxic thoughts that may have crept in yesterday or from your dreams. Each morning is the perfect opportunity for you to clear out the trash that may have become stuck inside your mind.

As you breathe, imagine any negative thoughts, fear, worries, or obstacles leaving your mind as you exhale. When you inhale, imagine yourself breathing in pure, clean, high-vibration light and love. See that light coming in with your breath and filling up your whole body.

The deeper you breathe, the more clarity you are bringing into your mind, heart, and body. Once you have done this breathing exercise for five to ten minutes, you will have a completely different perspective inside your mind. You will have more space to see the truth of how powerful you are at that very moment.

Now you are genuinely open to prayer and active listening for the will of your higher power, and you are ready to set your intention for the day.

Step 2: Affirm Your Mission Statement

Your mission statement is your guiding light that will make sure you stay on your path to achieving your purpose and never falling into a *Purpose Crisis* again.

It is best to read your mission statement first thing in the morning after you have done the breathing meditation exercise to clear your mind of any mind-clutter that may be distorting your focus. Once your mind is clear, create a mission statement for the day. It could be anything, but here are a couple of examples, "I will be kind and smile at everyone I see." or "I will embody love and abundance." Once you've decided on your mission statement repeat it three times out loud. It will become part of who you are.

When you say your mission statement out loud first thing in the morning when your mind is clear and your heart is open, you are infusing every cell of your body with the most powerful intention of your purpose. You will have more energy during your day because you will no longer feel lost or confused. You will find that you are able to establish your boundaries in loving ways within your relationships. You will be able to accomplish your goals faster and with more ease. It's all because you spent the most crucial time of the day — those first morning moments — programing your mind, both conscious and subconscious, to your highest purpose.

If we were taught how to practice this ritual in school, then perhaps most of us could have avoided the Purpose Crisis altogether. Regardless of what stage of life you are in now, you are ready to put this into action and see firsthand how this powerful the morning time will become your greatest ally in achieving your unique purpose.

Step 3: Hydrate

Hydration matters because, second to oxygen, water is the most essential nutrient for every cell in your body.

Water is essential, so I attempt to drink plenty of water every day. I admit that I have a tough time reaching my goal, but I still set the intention to drink at least 80 oz. of water each day. I've had to get creative by adding ingestible essential oils for flavor and added benefits or a squeeze or two of fresh lemon.

In the morning, I get a jumpstart on my hydration by drinking 16 oz. the moment I get out of bed. I love to add lemon because it boosts my immune system, balances my pH, aids in digestion, is a diuretic, clears my skin, and freshens my breath. A great way to start the day!

Step 4: Kickstart Your Nutrition

Eating a healthy, nutrient-dense breakfast refuels your body, enhances your mood, improves your concentration, helps you maintain a healthy weight, and is the foundation of a healthy diet for the balance of your day.

Usually, there is a fasting period of 8 to 12 hours between dinner and your morning meal. When you eat breakfast, you are breaking a fast from the night before. A lot of women skip eating breakfast because they are short on time, and this is destroying their metabolism. It can also create havoc with their hormones.

I start my day with a nutrition-dense shake and a personalized supplement plan.

(Visit JuliAnnStitick.com/MyFavoriteThings for all of my nutritional favorites).

An important thing to note here is that my supplements are correctly dialed in for me. I have my blood work taken every 6 months by a health practitioner or doctor to determine my hormone levels, vitamin deficiencies, mineral deficiencies, and even my stress levels. These supplements have been prescribed by the experts on my health optimization team, and we are continuously monitoring the effects of these supplements over the long term.

For you to find the perfect balance of vitamins, minerals, hormones and other internal balances that influence your metabolism, skin, and the health of your mind, you need to find a skilled practitioner that can analyze your blood work. It is only through this blood work analysis that you can indeed determine your specific needs.

Your nutrition plan should be whatever works for you. If you really want a challenge, eat sitting down and not standing at the sink (yep, I know you can do it!).

The key to nutrition is to make sure your brain and body are getting what they need to fuel you every day. When our bodies go into depletion of the important nutrients, everything begins to break down. When our bodies are breaking down, we will never have the energy or stamina to focus on our purpose.

There is no such thing as always being perfect with nutrition, but every day, you can make the intention that you are going to fuel your body with the nutrients that it needs for optimum health. But it's not enough to set the intention. You must make healthy choices along the way. Each and every action is a choice and you CAN make good choices, one at a time!

Step 5: Make Your Bed

Think of making your bed as a success habit. Although it may seem like a small task, it will give you a sense of accomplishment. Even better, it has been proven to reduce stress levels and increase your productivity. Your room will look tidy, and you will have developed a good habit.

When you make your bed in the morning, you have completed your first simple task of the day. That sets the tone for a day full of accomplishments. Plus, if someone pops by unannounced, you won't be embarrassed by your sloppy, unmade bed. Hey, it matters.

Step 6: Be Grateful

As I mentioned earlier in this book, developing an attitude of gratitude is one of the quickest ways to improve your mindset and your life. Gratitude may be one of the most overlooked practices we have access to in an instant.

Being grateful improves your physical health and psychological health. It is reported that grateful people tend to have fewer aches and pains, and feel healthier. Grateful people tend to exercise more often and take better overall care of their health. Appreciation for life increases happiness and reduces depression.

Each morning, whether it's in your Purpose Journal or an ongoing list on the mirror in your bathroom, write down 5 things you are grateful for. Later in the day you can take that a step further, and if you are thankful for someone in your life, tell them in person or shoot them a text!

I have been jotting my gratitude list on a poster-sized Post-it hanging on my wall. That way I have an in-my-face reminder to do it every day, so I never forget.

Step 7: Move Your Body

Morning is a great time to move your body! If you're anything like me, you may feel like Dorothy's Tin Man from *The Wizard of Oz* as you get your body out of bed — a little stiff and slow. A morning stretch and movement are essential for keeping me healthy and flexible. Then, it's time for one of the following: weight training, yoga, dancing, Pilates, or just a brisk walk with my dog, Lily. The trick is finding something you love to do.

When you exercise in the morning, you will consume fewer unnecessary calories, burn more fat, lower your blood pressure, and sleep better at night. Sounds good to me!

Step 8: Love Your Image

Now it's time to put yourself together for your day. Take the time to don an outfit you feel great about. Style your hair and makeup with the same care you would for a special occasion. Every day IS a special occasion to be cherished.

Once you're all dolled up, take a look in a full-length mirror and remind yourself to stand tall like the powerful woman you are (even if you're 5'1"). When you walk out the door, you will hold your head higher and interact with people more confidently and lovingly. They will notice a difference in you and treat you accordingly. You'll take bolder action, and that will lead you towards your purpose.

So, are you ready to begin this purpose-fueling Morning Routine? Can you make a commitment to YOU so that your needs can be at the top of the list? I know you can, but will you?
There's a beautiful side effect to feeling and looking vibrant. You deserve to feel your best. When you give yourself the time every day to refresh, renew, and nourish your body and spirit, it will be like adding to your purpose-fueling bank account.

This journey of self-care has been one of the most rewarding and challenging experiences of my life. It wasn't until I hit rock bottom that I really took a good hard look at how I wanted to live my life.

Going To Rehab

Let's talk about secrets. I had secrets when I was a child, and that compounded when I grew into an adult. I began to keep my excessive alcohol consumption to myself. I was ashamed. I vividly remember hiding it from my husband and my family, and I felt like a complete loser.

I took my first drink when I was fifteen years old — a glass of champagne at a wedding reception. I remember going home and feeling like I was floating on a cloud. I instantly loved it. When I drank, I was able to let down a little bit, and my body relaxed. I didn't have that self-loathing feeling.

I was a good kid in high school. I did a little bit of drinking but nothing major. It was the same with college, and finally, it progressed to the point that I started needing it. I would think, *"Not to worry. I could give it up if I needed to"*, but I never did. Ultimately, there was a moment that is still too painful for me to talk about that I realized I had a real problem.

I needed to stop, and I needed help. I went into an outpatient rehab program, and I got sober … for the first time.

I stayed sober for nine years. One day, I was visiting a friend in Colorado where all the guests were drinking beer. In an instant I picked up a beer, and I started right back up again.

It quickly got so bad that I didn't want my husband to know how much alcohol I was consuming. One night, I started cooking dinner and opened a bottle of wine that we were going to share. About a half hour before Joe was supposed to come home, I looked at the bottle and realized there was only about one glass left in the bottle. I did what any addicted person would do. I drank the rest of that bottle, and then I drove down to the store to get another bottle. Then I drank a glass out of that bottle because he would never believe that I had not had anything to drink because I smelled like alcohol. Craziness.

I don't condone any of the actions I took or ask for them to be excused because it's utterly unacceptable for someone to get behind the wheel of a car and drive after they've been drinking. I'm only grateful that nothing happened. By the grace of God, I didn't hurt someone else or myself.

I didn't recognize how sick it was. There was a moment when I stepped outside of myself, and I saw what was happening. I knew I couldn't do it any longer. Luckily, my family was still intact and I wasn't in trouble with the authorities as a result of my drinking. Nothing terrible had happened to me ...

yet. I knew that eventually; the other shoe was going to drop, and it terrified me.

Being an alcoholic gets very, very lonely. You can be surrounded by people all the time, but you still feel very much alone. You don't want to ask for help because you're embarrassed. There's a part of you that doesn't want to ask for help because you realize that when you ultimately do, you're going to be accountable.

If are struggling with an addiction and thinking, *"There's no way I could ever stop!"* then please take a deep breath. I know firsthand how hard it is to come face-to-face with a part of yourself that you're not proud of. That's the turning point. Maybe that's today, and perhaps it's not. Wherever you are, first and foremost, please, ask for help. Everything is going to be okay because you will always, today and forever, know that you do have a choice. In January of 2006, I quit drinking for good, and I haven't had a drink since. My life is much better now.

Maybe you're reading this, and alcohol isn't your addiction. Perhaps it's something else like food, sex, drama, or shopping. There are all types of addictions. What it comes down to is there is either a chemical imbalance going on that needs healing. There's a psychological or a mental deficit that needs professional support. There's an emotional deficit. That can sometimes be the most debilitating because we're trying to fill the hole in our soul with something outside of connecting with God or our purpose. It's important to know that you are not a "bad" person, and there is help out there for you.

When you are seeking to fill this void inside of you with something that is outside of you, you will never reach the end. You may get a temporary high that feels complete, for a moment, but it will never last. This is why addictions are so dangerous to our emotional balance. They lift us up so high and then crash us down even further than before. To get to that level of high again, you have to consume more and more. Every time, the crash is harder than the last. It's a downward spiral.

Please seek help if you are aware that you are struggling with any kind of an addiction. As a person who recognizes that I am an addict, I have found that the only way out of loneliness and the misery of addiction is to ask for support and rely on my higher power. You don't have to do this alone.

I am living proof that you can overcome even your darkest demons. That void inside of me could only be filled by searching for and connecting with something greater than myself.

The fact that I no longer drink doesn't mean that the addiction tendency has completely gone away. I am who I am and I've found peace with how my mind works today. Instead of trying to fight against my natural tendencies, I take that hyper-focused energy and point it at something meaningful and productive, like serving others.

Sobriety has impacted my life in many different ways. Now that I have a clear head to make good choices, I have less drama around me. I don't have the show in my life anymore. Now, I view the things that would've caused me to fall apart in the past as life circumstances. Circumstances I can meet head-on because I have the tools I need to do so in a healthy way.

When I first got sober, I was asked to write about what my dreams were for my life. When I look at that now, I realize I was selling myself short. When I show up every day as a healthy, responsible adult, and do my best job for every task that's in front of me, that's when magic happens.

The confidence builds so I feel more equipped to take even greater risks. They're healthy risks that allow me to stretch myself to new levels. To be completely honest, the journey continues to this day.

Perhaps you are on the precipice of letting go of some addiction that is no longer welcome in your life, and you were called to this book at exactly the right time. If I can send a wish your way, I hope that you will receive this.

Find one person who truly wants what's best for you, someone you know will support you in the process, and ask for help. It's that first step of asking for help that is a step towards success. Get the support you need, whether it's admitting yourself to rehab or going to a support group. There are many programs that can help you with your addiction so you don't have to do it on your own.

Today there's so much more awareness than when I first got sober. I don't think there's the same level of shame as there was in the past. Now, so many people are openly talking about their struggles with addiction. When I meet someone else in recovery, there is an instant kinship. It's almost like you instantly get each other. That's why group programs are so effective because you feel like you know one another, even if you've only just met.

Initially, when I got sober, it was one minute at a time or indeed one *ugh* at a time. After a while, it became part of my life, or I should say, no longer part of my life. I know there's not even an option for me to drink again. I know that if I pick up one drink, I will pick up ten. There's no going back to that. Frankly, it's kind of nice to be somebody who doesn't drink because I always feel good in the morning. I never have hangovers. I'm no longer bloated or puffy. I'm no longer skipping proper nutrition for a glass of wine.

I'm also getting my excitement and enthusiasm from other places. I search for that joy in different ways. I don't need to drink to have fun. That's when you know you've overcome it. You do not need to be owned by your addiction.

When I first quit drinking, I would hear people say that they were grateful alcoholics. I used to think that they had lost their marbles. What I now know is that I am thankful that my addiction brought me to a place where I learned some very critical tools for living my life, and those are the 12 Steps.

Now that I have those 12 Steps in my life toolbox, every time I am faced with a challenge, I'm able to look at that challenge and say, *"What step can I apply here?"* What's beautiful is I don't have broken relationships in my life anymore. I'm not always trying to clean up a mess. My life is much more serene.

8

Purpose Boundaries

"For what shall it profit a man, if he gains the whole world, and suffer the loss of his soul?"
- Jesus Christ

I love boundaries. I wasn't always good at them, and that is incredibly common in women. I was not clear how to stand up for myself because my boundaries were scrambled. Today, I've learned that the more I create boundaries, the more I honor and respect myself. I set loving limits so that people are clear about how to treat me.

Often, I think people are afraid to set boundaries because they believe that this will cause friction with their loved ones. But the exact opposite is true. You will find that when you are clear with your loved ones about what you want and need, they ultimately feel more relaxed with you.

The Rule of Threes

One of my favorite exercises for setting boundaries is what I call The Rule of Threes. When you are trying to establish a limit with someone, this can be a powerful and loving way to do it. Let's say there's a conversation that you need to have, and you're not quite ready to have it. The other individual is pushing you to have this conversation, but you know you're not prepared for it. Rather than complying and having the conversation before you feel like you're emotionally grounded, you can use the Rule of Threes — in essence, repeating yourself three times.

1. You say from a place of power and compassion, *"I really do want to have this conversation. I'm not ready, but I will come back to you when I am."* Then, if the other person persists saying, *"Well, I think we need to talk about this, now."*

2. Calmly repeat yourself and say, *"I hear what you're saying, but I'm not ready to have this conversation yet. I promise that when I am, I will get back to you."*

3. If this person comes back a third time, repeat the same thing very calmly, and 99% of the time people will back off.

You don't have to get upset, and it doesn't have to turn into an argument. It's merely repeating what is right for you, three times.

Practice the Rule of Threes the next time someone is trying to pressure you to do something that you are not ready to or don't want to do. Stand firm in repeating where you are three times. They will then see they cannot break your boundary, and they will actually have more respect for you when you do finally chat about it!

The other reason that boundaries are so important is that it keeps you from forming resentments towards people. I often hear people complaining, *"This person did this to me,"* and *"this person did that to me."* The truth is that, when we don't put the boundaries in place, it ultimately ends up being our responsibility when we are choosing to feel annoyed or irritated with how others are treating us. When we are not willing to set loving limits, we are not keeping our side of the street clean in that relationship.

Setting boundaries may mean limiting the amount of time you spend with family members with whom you don't get along. That is also a loving boundary.

A loving boundary is sometimes just saying no. It's hard for many women to say no. When I started saying no, it became something I actually enjoyed doing. Now I'm able to say, *"I'm happy you think I would be suitable for this job, but it's not right for me at this time. Thank you so much for asking."* I know I would ultimately end up being resentful or overwhelmed if I took the role just because I felt bad turning someone down. When I receive an invitation like this from someone I ask myself, *"Is this something that I'm going to be excited to be a part of? Am I doing it because I think I need to say yes so I can make somebody else happy? Would I be neglecting what is best for me?"*

Setting clear boundaries will protect and fuel your purpose all at the same time!

If this is new to you, we are going to take this in baby steps. This is some of the most important work you can do to protect your purpose in the long run.

We need to establish what your limitations are.

Let's say you meet someone at a business networking event, and as that relationship grows, you begin to recognize this person is not in alignment with you. You might see traits you do not respect. It's so subtle that it takes you a while to figure it out. The boundary here would be to decide not to continue that relationship or limit your exposure to that person. Surround yourself with people who you respect and admire. Spend your time with people who want the best for you and share your values.

When we have boundaries, we are honoring our purpose. There are two ways that we are accepting our mission from our highest self. The first is that we are protecting it from being affected by people who may not be in alignment with our purpose. They may distract us from our purpose. This is where we are protecting our purpose from the outside. Think of it as a bubble around your purpose.

Then, there's our internal boundary — something created within us. We're saying, *"This purpose is sacred to me and I'm going to honor my purpose first."* When we have clear internal boundaries, we start every day setting an intention that we are living our purpose. It's establishing that alignment with our rituals, a morning meditation, or a mission statement. That's creating that inner boundary of holding your purpose sacred — like that compass, that true north. So, we check in with our purpose, and we align every intention.

Can you see there are two different ways we need to establish these boundaries? There's the bubble around us that's not letting anyone in, and then there's also that boundary inside of us that's preventing us from being pulled off purpose.

Other Boundaries in Your Life

This reminds me of another boundary I've set up: the boundary that I set around not watching the news. I don't want to hear it, read it or talk about it. I will quietly remove myself from any situation where people are discussing negative topics that are not pertinent to what I determine is crucial for me to know.

143

I almost see it as a wall. The Great Wall of China was a boundary to keep the invaders out, and it also protected the people within it.

One of the reasons I don't want to watch the news or talk about divisive issues is that I have explicit beliefs in my life. One of those beliefs is that my feelings are mine, and it is not my responsibility to have anyone conform to my ideas, or what I choose to believe. Knowing about all of the negativity going on in the world does not foster a healthy lifestyle for me, and it undoubtedly does not fuel my purpose.

In many ways, we are living in one of the most abundant periods in our history, but you would never know it by watching the media. I consider the news a dangerous distraction. If I need to know the weather report, I'll merely check my weather app. If there is something I should know that is crucial to my day-to-day existence, I can be informed by a trusted friend or family member.

This boundary protects my purpose. When I am protected from constant negativity, I am able to stay on course and be in a much better state of mind to live my purpose through every daily interaction.

I'd rather eat the elephant one bite at a time. Maybe that's a strange way of saying it, but what I mean is that I take baby steps to make the world a better place every day by how I treat every human being I encounter. If I am upset and stressed about circumstances beyond my control, if affects my mood. Only when I am at my best can I make a difference, one connection at a time.

It all comes back to the purpose, right? Once we know our purpose, it's easy to disregard the distractions and stay on target. The purpose is our compass. Anything that's outside of the boundary of your purpose won't serve you, and it won't help humanity. The purpose is what we're honoring with our actions and what we're allowing into our psyche. When we're clear on our purpose, we can say yes to what we want and no to what is not right for us.

Your Point of Purpose

You've probably never heard boundaries expressed in this way. I think it's essential to talk about this because the term boundaries has been thrown around a lot.

Sometimes people use boundaries to hurt other people. That's not we're talking about here. Let's go back to Walsh's quote, *"the intention of the soul"* or my version, *"How does this point to my purpose?"* What we are saying is that you use boundaries to protect yourself, to make sure that how you show up in the world is authentically in alignment with your purpose. These boundaries allow you to be the best version of yourself.

I love teaching my clients how to create loving boundaries and how it is essential to achieving their goals and dreams. Many people don't know how to say, *"No."* We literally have to work on it. A lot of women think they have to come up with the perfect way to say no to something. This puts unnecessary pressure on them when instead they can calmly and simply decline and honor their worth.

When somebody asks me to take on a role and it's not on purpose for me, I will just respond by saying, *"I am so honored and touched that you invited me and wanted me. I'm not able to say yes. I know that you will find the right person. If you'd like me to keep this in the back of my mind to help you find that right person, I will be happy to do that, but as for me being that person, the answer is no."* By honoring that they thought of you, you are keeping the relationship whole while still declaring the boundary. You're very clear about the fact that it's not on purpose for you. Then you are offering a solution in helping them find someone that will be the right person for the role.

Here's another thing about saying no. When someone makes a request, you can push the pause button. Give yourself the opportunity to sleep on it and ask a friend or mentor if you can run it past them if need be. When we make impulsive decisions and give spontaneous answers just because we think we need to, we are not honoring our boundaries. In turn, this ends up hurting everyone in the long run.

People may not like it at first but will actually respect you more when you set these loving boundaries. They'll appreciate the response when you own the solution. The tone of voice that you use when you make the delivery needs to be very grounded, bright, and resolute.

That's where that Rule of Threes comes into play again. It's empowering to be able to know, in advance, what you will say when someone asks you to do something that is not in alignment with your purpose.

People Pleasing

When women are people pleasers, they have a hard time asserting their boundaries because they want everyone to be happy. They don't want anyone to be upset with them. Deep down, I believe we all feel that way at heart. I do. I guess we want to be able to be everything to everyone at some level. Many of us have a childhood wound that has wired us that way. A big part of a woman asserting her boundaries is coming to terms with the fact that not everybody is going to like her or be happy with her all the time.

At their core, people are looking for affirmation from others, meaning that they're liked by other people so this validates that they are worthy of love. Some people fill this void by achieving something — a win or a trophy. Others are driven by power. They want to have control over other people, and that gives them a fleeting sense of worth. People pleasers want to be liked and popular, and that can be the driving force behind everything they do.

People pleasers say yes without authentically meaning it, and then they don't follow through with their intention. It leaves the relationship in a confused state. You aren't ever confident when this person agrees to something if it is something they genuinely want, versus committing just to make you happy. This creates a breakdown in trust.

There's no boundary within that person. It can get frustrating because when they don't follow through it's because their heart wasn't in it to start with, and now there's tension or even a broken relationship as a result.

A relationship is like cake batter. Each party is putting ingredients into that cake batter, and that is the recipe for the relationship. When you begin to change the ingredients you put into the cake batter, it changes the entire cake.

Your relationships have the opportunity to be healthier because you've put healthier ingredients into that relationship "batter" by establishing boundaries and not being a people pleaser. Be gentle and patient with yourself as you start to awaken to new possibilities and let go of people-pleasing mentality. Usually, this has been a lifetime habit that needs time to change.

The Purpose Litmus Test

This exercise is simple and powerful. The next time someone asks you to do something, whether it's your kids begging you to pick up a special lunch because they forgot theirs, yet again, or your co-worker inviting you out for a drink when you don't feel like going, you're going to check in with yourself before you answer them. You're going to run the litmus test:

    A. Is this something that is going to fuel my purpose?
    B. Is this something that I'm too tired or overwhelmed to do?
    C. Do I already have enough on my plate and want to avoid overloading myself?

That will be your litmus test.

When you let go of people pleasing, you can tap into the truth that is always inside of you, waiting to be seen and heard. More often than not, people understand when you say no. If they don't respect your boundary, then maybe you don't want them in your life. It may be as simple as that.

It's a final opportunity to say, *"Thank you for the offer. I'm going to decline because I'm just not up for it."* Who can argue with that?

9

Purpose Contribution - Giving From Abundance

"No one saves us but ourselves. No one can, and no one may. We must walk the path."
- Buddha

Giving from abundance is an essential step in staying on your purpose and staying out of a Purpose Crisis. I see the world as not just half-empty, or half-full, but overflowing all the time. All we have to do is look for it.

I look at virtually every situation in life and ask, *"How can I contribute?"* Often when people think of contribution, they think of a monetary donation to an organization, and it stops there. They don't ever participate in their day-to-day life.

There are ways to contribute everywhere you go and, in every moment, if you choose to look at it that way. It may be when I'm checking out at the grocery store, and I strike up a conversation with the checker. I get to know the names of her children and where they are attending college. No doubt when someone takes an interest in her beyond asking for a price check, it is a way of contributing. It is a contribution of being seen, understood, and heard by a fellow human.

A contribution could be looking at a homeless man in the eye, smiling at him, and saying hello. It could be taking the time to speak to the housekeeper at your hotel and giving her an extra tip. It could be baking a pie every Wednesday.

Pies for Heroes

For the last year, I have baked a pie, every single Wednesday. Even five days after I had spine surgery, I still baked that pie. I deliver these pies to my local fire station, Pasadena Fire Department, Station 31.

I began by delivering homemade pies to various service organizations throughout my local community. The firehouse was my fourth stop on this pie-making tour.

When I dropped off my first pie and explained my mission, the captain immediately placed a special order for fresh blueberry the next week. These firemen decided to adopt me and have become my friends. They make special requests and even vote on their favorites. They've also given me a VIP, "Very Important Pie Maker" parking spot, right behind the station. Each week I look forward to delivering a pie and making them feel appreciated. I love to bake and share it with others, so this contribution serves both!

Local Community Contribution

How can you contribute to your local community? No action is too small. There are people in your neighborhood that you can support or make their day easier in some way. It starts the day that you decide to do it, and the rewards will come back to you one thousand-fold.

Global Contribution

This book is one of my global contributions. My goal is to reach a billion and one women across the globe with this message. It is my mission to help them get out of the Purpose Crisis that is devastating their self-esteem and preventing them from living their most fulfilling life possible.

How will this impact the world globally? I believe people are born with a purpose. It's part of them just like the color of their hair, the shade of their skin, or their tone of voice. Since we are born with that purpose, that purpose is pure, and it's full of love. It's innocent. When we can, as a global community, get closer to living our purpose every day, we will affect the world in a way that is organic, loving and far-reaching.

By helping one billion and one women to get out of their Purpose Crisis, I will be able to serve our global community because those women will do it at a higher level. They will be better mothers, better friends, and better leaders. They will have more joy in their lives, and in turn, will want to support other women. It's one candle lighting another — candles that will ultimately illuminate the globe.

That is my purpose — I want to eradicate the Purpose Crisis and share this light with as many women as possible.

In sharing these gifts, women will have more to contribute to their families and loved ones. It will trickle down to the younger generations that are the future of our world.

When one billion and one women wake up to their real purpose, and we eliminate the *Purpose Crisis* on the planet, the next generation of women will never even search for their purpose because they will already know it. They will have role models, and examples of women who are living on purpose. The crisis will be over.

Going through this book and doing the action steps together awakens our unique purpose within us. We, the collective we, everyone who's on this mission with us, are all coming together as one dominant, unstoppable force. We are alleviating the planet of this plague, this disease that is the *Purpose Crisis*.

Our contribution to ourselves is supporting one another and also helping the future generation.

That's why the most significant gift we can ever give is this contribution we give to ourselves by fueling our purpose. The act of giving yourself this gift shows others that abundance is high, and the cup of contribution is flowing over.

ACTION STEP: Global Contribution

How Does Your Purpose Serve A Higher Good Locally? Globally? Answer these questions in your Purpose Journal.

You Cannot Quit... Ever

As women, we are prone to be inconsistent about the very things we need most. We are so focused on taking care of everyone else, and when we do things for ourselves, we feel guilty about it. We start to think that either the financial resources, or time, or energy should be going towards other people and not to us.

Women often tell me they think it's selfish to focus on themselves and their dreams. Unfortunately, many women role models exhaust their energies serving others and forget about helping themselves. We all know that having a heart of service for others is admirable, but doesn't that go both ways? This is a crucial obstacle that we must overcome to eliminate the Purpose Crisis forever.

Women who nurture their purpose are setting a most potent example for younger women. Even if that means they can't go to every single volleyball game or dance recital. If they are out living their life independently of the caretaker role, and their daughter, or niece, or friend sees they are living their best experience possible, this becomes the example. When you serve yourself you encourage your loved ones to nurture their purpose, as well.

It goes along with that saying, *"Kids won't do what you say, they do what you do."* To indeed be the best role model is for you to live your message. As Gandhi says, *"My life is my message."*

Shoes for the Homeless

My mother was one of those people that lived on purpose and kept her eyes open to the needs of the less fortunate every single day. One day we were sitting at a red light, and a homeless gentleman walked across the street in front of us. The soles of his shoes were flapping because they had holes in them. My Mother said, *"You know, I think your Dad might have a pair of tennis shoes that he's not wearing. If they're the right size, I would love to give them to him."*

Time went on, and she never saw the man again, but it sparked an idea in her. She supposed that, like my dad, many people probably had an extra pair of tennis shoes sitting in their closet — shoes they didn't wear. My mother, God bless her, sent a letter to our local newspaper, basically saying, if you have an extra pair of tennis shoes even if they're dirty, please drop them off at 610 W. Broadway in Glendale on my front porch. The following week we had close to 300 pairs of shoes.

Some people had bought brand new shoes! My mother then lovingly and painstakingly put new shoelaces in the shoes that needed them replaced. She washed the shoes that needed washing and ultimately gifted them to a homeless shelter.

I vividly remember the photograph in the newspaper when they reported the outcome of my mother's outreach. She was sitting in a pile of 300 shoes in the middle of our living room. That impacted me. It reminded me that I could make a difference, too. It was a culture that I grew up with, and it's straightforward when you see it. You look around you, and you see where's there's a need, and you help.

My sweet mother, Judy Cash, taught me about the impact of helping others in need. I'm forever grateful that both parents opened up the possibilities for me to seek and find my purpose through their contribution to others.

ACTION STEP: Your Role Model for Contribution

In your Purpose Journal write about a role model who set the 'contribution' example for you and describe how they impacted your beliefs.

10

Purpose Play

"There is one quality which one must possess to win, and that is definiteness of purpose, the knowledge of what one wants, and a burning desire to possess it."
- Napoleon Hill

We want to keep this whole serious business of "finding your purpose" light and fun. In order to do that, it's important to see it as a game. The most vital match you will ever play. Why is a game so important for finding your purpose and staying on target?

It's because it's fun and it's mandatory for us to have a balance in our lives in order to live a purpose-driven life. Part of that balance is having fun and tapping into our childlike spirit. We need to stop taking life quite so seriously. We need to go on adventures, even if it's jumping in the car on a Friday night and saying, *"Where should we go to dinner? Let's go to a new town, drive around, and see what grabs our attention."*

Another adventure could be flying on a trapeze, jumping off the platform, swinging on the swing and waiting for someone on the other end to catch you in midair. Adventures of play fuel your soul.

We have to find the things that fuel our souls. If it's in nature, find experiences to get out and smell the fresh air. If it's traveling to big cities and window shopping that feeds you, then that's what you need to do. If it's playing beach volley ball with your friends, then that's your adventure. I look at every part of life as a possibility for adventure. If we decide to look at it that way, it changes our search for our purpose.

When life's journey hits us in the face, we can begin to view it as an adventure, *"Here's another adventure in life. How am I going to work through this so that I can grow, and I can handle it in a way that I feel incredibly proud of myself?"* When you see obstacles as part of the adventure, then you meet them with more grace to dance through the difficult times.

Adventure also sparks creativity. When our creative juices are flowing, we become more adept at finding ways to live our purpose. Finding ways to challenge ourselves and ask, *"How can I take this adventure and point it to the target?"*

Let's go back to the example with the trapeze. I won a prize with my business mentor, Allison Maslan, for a full day of business coaching plus trapeze lessons. Did I mention I'm afraid of heights? When I was waiting to climb the ladder, I was thinking, *"You are crazy. You should not be doing this. You're going to fall. You're going to hurt yourself."*

I caught myself in this self-defeating loop of negative thinking. I decided to look at it from a different angle. I asked myself, *"How can I point this to my purpose?"* Answer... living on purpose takes courage, and it can be scary at times.

We have many fears in our lives. We have many limitations that sit on our shoulders and tell us we shouldn't or can't do something. There are so many reasons to think it's not ok? The only thing you can do to stop these self-defeating thoughts is to jump, to jump high and hard. You have to jump off the platform. To take that first leap, you have to remember that this is what points to the purpose.

There are going to be times when it's terrifying. I stood on the edge of the trapeze platform with my toes curled over the end, leaning entirely out over open space. When I was reaching for the swing, there was that moment of, *"You are crazy."* I made a decision right then and there that this was something I wanted to accomplish because it was going to help me grow as an individual and at the same time, point me closer to my purpose. I leaned out with my body straight and hips forward. I listened to the instructor. I followed his directions, and I felt fantastic about what I had achieved just 90 minutes later. I could have climbed Mt. Everest (not really, it's too cold there, but you get the idea).

That play allowed me to find something inside of myself I would have missed if I was taking life too seriously. I would never have overcome my fear of heights. I took it on like it was a playful adventure, and now I've mastered this fear that I thought was impenetrable and would never budge. When we are playful and adventurous, we step outside of this rigid definition of who we are and who we're supposed to be. It is outside of the labels and fears that we get closer to aligning with our real purpose.

Oh and by the way, the most significant injury I sustained was a ripped toenail. Yeah. It's not pretty. I ripped my toenail big time, and I'm thinking, *"Oh this is going to take weeks of not wearing sandals until my toenail grows back out. And it's happening at the worst time because spring and summer are just around the corner."* It's all about how the feet look in the shoes! Quality problem (ha).

ACTION STEP: Face Your Fear

In your Purpose Journal write 5 things that scare you. Now, choose one of them and make a plan to tackle that personal challenge! You can do it.

Unlimited You Exercise Revisited

Remember that first exercise we did together way back at the beginning of this book? We are going to do it again. Now that you have done the work of discovering your purpose, you have more clarity of what that means. You will be amazed at all the changes that have occurred simply by turning these pages and taking action.

ACTION STEP: The Unlimited You Exercise

The Unlimited YOU Exercise

We want to describe each of these in detail:

1. What are your ideal relationships like? (partner, kids, family, friends, etc.) Writing down an answer rather than just thinking it through will give you the most significant impact in finding your purpose. In other words, write it down doll.

2. What is your perfect environment? (home, work, free time, etc.)

3. What is your health like? (energy levels, sleeping, mental clarity, happiness levels, etc.)

4. What is your business or career like in your perfect vision? (how much income, how many employees, work from home or commute to an office, etc.)

5. What are your hobbies? (free time activities, travel, community involvement, sports, and recreation, etc.)

6. What are you doing for fun? (dinner dates, hanging out with your friends, family time, creative art projects, etc.)

7. How are you contributing to the world? (philanthropy, charity, volunteering, non-profit, fundraising, etc.)

JuliAnn Stitick

The Personal Brand Expert

PurposeCrisis.com

Putting Yourself Out There in a Bigger Way

"Fortune favors the bold."
- Virgil

Writing this book has been yet another giant step towards living my purpose. As I search my heart, my soul, and my experiences, it is a reminder that I'm on my perfect path, yet I've still got a long way to go.

That's the exciting thing! I already feel like I am living on purpose. At the same time, as I explore all these different aspects of pointing to purpose, I recognize there's room for growth in every single one of them.

As a woman on a mission to create a movement with one billion and one women, it's incredibly important for me to be as real, authentic and transparent as possible. I'm never done learning and I'm never done growing.

Thank you for taking this journey with me to grow closer to your purpose. As we create the movement of one billion and one women waking up to experience their highest life purpose, you will see the world change for the better. When there are one billion women who are awakened to their unique purpose, that will be the turning point to make sure the Purpose Crisis will be eradicated forever. That one extra woman is for extra measure to make sure that we are always moving forward, and forever expanding our reach to the new horizons that lie in the distance.

I am counting on you to help spread this message so if this book has impacted you in any way, I am challenging you to tell three women about *Purpose Crisis.* Better yet, gift them a book of their own and start a book club.

If you are looking for a group of motivated, inspiring, and heart-centered women that are here to support you in your journey of living your life with your greatest purpose, then I have a special invitation for you. Please join *"The Women of Purpose"*. You don't have to go it alone. The more support we give to other women on this journey, the more we are able to share and contribute our greatest gifts. Join us at www.TheWomenOfPurpose.com.

We have yet to experience a world where women are fully in tune with their innate gifts and aligned with their purpose. Once we get there, we need to make sure that we never, ever stop striving for a deeper discovery of our soul.

I love you, and in the next horizon of our awakening, I will meet you there.

References

Cohen, Jennifer. 'Busy vs. Productive: Which One Are You?' *Forbes Online Magazine.* 2018. https://www.forbes.com/sites/jennifercohen/2018/06/25/busy-vs-productive-which-one-are-you/#24163bf7d798

Levine, Kenneth. Muenchen, Robert. Brooks, Abby. *Measuring Transformational and Charismatic Leadership: Why isn't Charisma Measured?* Taylor and Francis Online. 2010. https://www.tandfonline.com/doi/abs/10.1080/03637751.2010.499368

Toussaint, Loren L., Owen, Amy, Cheadle, Alyssa. Forgive to Live: Forgiveness, Health and Longevity. Journal of Behavioral Medicine (2010). ISSN 0160-7715. http://www.academia.edu/1007805/Forgive_to_Live_Forgiveness_Health_and_Longevity

Walsh, Neil Donald. *Conversations With God.* Los Angeles: Hodder Paperback, 1997.